P9-DCR-954

BETWEEN PARENTS AND GRANDPARENTS

ARTHUR
KORNHABER, M.D.

Between Parents and Grandparents

ST. MARTIN'S PRESS / New York

 For information, address St. Martin's Press, 175 Fifth Avenue, New York, N.Y. 10010.

Design by Laura Hough

Library of Congress Cataloging-in-Publication Data
Kornhaber, Arthur.
Between parents and grandparents.
1. Parent and child. 2. Grandparent and child.
3. Family—Psychological aspects. I. Title.
HQ755.85.K67 1986 306.8'7 86–1950
ISBN 0-312-07734-3

First Edition
10 9 8 7 6 5 4 3 2 1

For my dear wife Carol
. . . a "natural"

Contents

PART I

Birthright and Legacy: Why It's Important

ONE

Who Dreams About Becoming a Grandparent?

There are three times when our lives are totally transformed by natural events without our having much to say about it: when we are born, when we die, and when we become grandparents.

Today people are willing to talk a great deal about birth and death, but most of us ignore our roles as grandchildren and grandparents. This is a tragic state of affairs. As a child psychiatrist and researcher who has been studying this issue for over a decade, I can state categorically that a healthy and loving bond between grandparents and grandchildren is necessary for the emotional health and happiness of all three generations. This bond is a natural birthright for children, realized through an emotional attachment, a legacy bequeathed by their elders that benefits everyone in the family. Unfortunately, family members are increasingly being deprived of the benefits of this relationship. Why is this happening?

First, most people are unaware of the significance of intergenerational relationships. Second, the unigenerational structure of modern society—people primarily spending their time within their own age group—and the rapid tempo of our lives mitigates against the formation of vital connections and deep, enduring, emotional attachments. These factors are so powerful that even people who do recognize the importance of close generational ties find it difficult to make it happen for them. They can't overcome the social and personal obstacles that they find between their loved ones and themselves.

Not only is the job of grandparenting kept under wraps, so is the thought of it, even the idea. Grandparenting is not anticipated in the same way that people look forward to becoming a parent or embarking upon their chosen career. Who dreams about becoming a grandparent?

THE SILENCE

Today, not only are people of all generations unwilling to put forth the effort to nurture, to "garden" emotional attachments, they seem to go out of their way to isolate themselves from one another, even within their own families.

Among busy individuals of all ages, who are just barely coping with their harried lives, there is a consensus that there is already too much to do. Children are isolated from elders in schools and caretaking institutions. Young adults have little time for their elders, even if they have an interested adult who is eager to be with them. The thought that one day they, the youngsters, might become grandparents never enters their minds. The middle generation is walking a tightrope between earning a living and raising a family, and perhaps supporting their own parents, and they have little interest in what's happening between their parents and their children—unless they are among the fortunate few whose parents help with their everyday burdens. Parents rarely think about the time when they too will become grandparents. And for grandparents who work, who have moved away in retirement, or who live down the street but who aren't interested, the less said about it, the better. The very subject makes them feel guilty.

Better to keep silent.

It's not only inconvenient but annoying for some people to consider the results of their actions beyond one generation. Do retiring grandparents want to think about the sad grandchildren who cannot understand why their beloved grandparents left them? Do parents want to bother to consider the effects of their divorce and remarriage on their parents? What does this mean but more grandparents to deal with, more pressures to get the kids and grandparents together, more driving, more holiday presents, more hassles, more work? It's easier to sweep it all under the rug.

What about great-grandma and great-grandpa? Is it "cost effective" to keep them alive? Are they not a burden to their children? Shall they not be "put away," with guilt for all, because there is no time or interest to care for them?

Why should grandparents break the silence? Portraying themselves as passive victims of their children's rejection is a safe way to keep to themselves. True, institutions and professions ignore the importance of grandparent participation because it's just too much trouble to deal with. True, the law may even legislate grandparents out of existence when their grandchild's custodian (sometimes their very own child) doesn't want them around. True, some grandparents are rejected by their own children. True, grandparents deserve a bit of time for themselves after their children grow up.

Who is rejecting whom?

The silence continues unbroken even though the extended family is being torn apart at an ever accelerating pace. The "advances" the new generation has enjoyed have been paid for with a terrible emotional price. There is a curious paradox occurring. The extended family is getting larger and broader, with more people of different ages, at the same time that its members are splitting off from one another and leaving their families to spend their lives doing business in the impersonal world outside of the family confines. More and more youngsters are being given to paid professionals to raise as their mothers leave home, out of need or desire, for the workplace. Men's newfound and overdue interest in childrearing will not compensate kids for the lack of a mother. It seems that anyone who can, flees home; it's become a hallmark of our times. Too many people prefer to "hang out" exclusively with people of the same age. Young people know few elders. They are not learning how to be old;

they are learning that their elders do not care to spend time with them. How are they going to feel in the future when they will be obligated to spend their hard-earned dollars to support a growing elderly population of anonymous and "useless" old people? Not very generous, I imagine.

ENDING THE SILENCE

Shall we perpetuate the silence? If not, who's going to make the necessary changes?

The answer to these questions must be emphatic. Changes are possible, and we are the people to make them. We are the generation of parents and grandparents who have just come upon the scene. We can end the silence.

The New Generation

A new generation of elders is appearing in the "advanced" countries of the world. The beneficiaries of social and medical progress, they are long-lived, healthy, educated, and more economically secure than at any other time in recorded history. Within a decade, their children will be grandparents. In the near future, four-generation families will become more commonplace. Today, over seventy percent of the people over sixty-five are grandparents. It is projected that nearly one-half of today's grandparents will live to become great-grandparents.

Simply becoming grandparents can open creative floodgates for elders to use the gift of time, health, and vitality, and gain the love and respect that they deserve. Also, it can earn them a vital place in the hearts of their loved ones and an important role in their communities. Shared with parents, the linchpin of the connection between grandparents and grandchildren, this role enriches all their lives and assures the continuity of the family. This is the greatest gift of all.

But is there a best way to use this gift? Yes: to start when this new family comes into being, when the new grandchild is born. This is the unique opportunity this book has been written to foster and to celebrate. Motivated parents and grandparents can learn about the pleasures and pain of the three- and four-generational relationship and learn to use this knowledge to identify conflicts, prevent new problems, and repair existing ones.

With this knowledge, the new generation of grandparents can use their gift most effectively, fulfilling the birthright of the young in a relationship with them, and assuring that their legacy is received and passed on to future generations. With this legacy comes a hope and a dream. The hope is that the new generation can forge a fulfilling and happy life. The dream is that someday their own children will look forward to becoming grandparents.

TWO

What's Special About the Grandparent–Grandchild Bond?

In 1975, with my colleagues, I began to investigate the nature of the grandparent-grandchild relationship. My interest stemmed not only from the love and attention of my own grandparents, but because of a clinical encounter with a youngster named Billy.

When I first met Billy, he was an immature child at odds with this world. Neither his parents, teachers, friends nor relatives understood him, he said, only his grandparents. "Everybody always looks mad at me except them." And when I first saw Billy in my office with his grandparents, he was transformed. Instead of sulking, he engaged in good-natured conversation. Instead of being inattentive, surly, and negative, he was cheerful, outgoing, and cooperative.

Reflecting upon this apparent miracle, I asked my other young patients about their grandparents. To my surprise, most of the children hardly knew them. After reading whatever literature I could find on the subject (and discovering that, indeed, not much existed), I decided to embark on a systematic study of the nature of this relationship. I wanted to answer some questions: What, if anything, is special about the relationship between parents and grandparents? How does it work? Who does it effect? Does it matter? With my wife Carol as research collaborator, I traveled the country interviewing grandparents, parents, and grandchildren to learn about their perceptions and feelings toward one another. For the adults, we used a research questionnaire, followed by a long personal interview. We asked the youngsters to draw a picture of a grandparent, and then talked to them about the picture and their "real" grandparent. After three years and interviews with three hundred subjects, we completed the first phase of the study and published our findings, with Kenneth L. Woodward as collaborator, in a book entitled *Grandparents/Grandchildren—The Vital Connection.*

Our study showed that the grandparent-grandchild bond mattered very much. It is second only in emotional power to the parent-child bond. Grandparents and grandchildren affect each other very deeply—for better or worse—just because they exist. Parents also affect the grandparent-grandchild relationship. They benefit when a close emotional attachment exists between their parents and their children. We also learned that miseries passed on from grandparent to parent are not directly passed on from grandparent to grandchild, although children can assume their parents' negative attitudes toward their grandparents if they don't spend enough time with the grandparents to make a decision for themselves.

Nature gives grandparents another chance.

GRANDCHILDREN

Not only were children with close grandparents more rooted in their families and communities, they felt very emotionally secure. They mattered to people. They had many people who were crazy about them. They were not ageist, and they loved old people. Indeed, many of these children looked forward to being old themselves because of the loving role model that their grandparents offered. Because of their grandparents, they had a place to go and someone to comfort them, someone to listen to their problems and offer advice—an emotional sanctuary. When they had difficulties with their parents, such children had someone to intercede for them with their parents—the "boss's boss," as one youngster said. Because their grandparents had lived in another era, such children often knew other languages, other values, and other ways of thinking. We call this "social immunity"—a process whereby children gain knowledge beyond the everyday teachings of their society. Learning through their grandparents' stories and examples, such children are not dependent on only their own historical era to understand the world. They learn about history firsthand, from people who were there. They learned how events *felt.* Children with close grandparents feel that they *belong* to a group, their family, and that their behavior reflects upon the family. They are not alone, and do not perceive themselves to be in isolation. They speak of their families in collective terms as "we." Their families have a specific personality comprised of shared attitudes and behaviors. One youngster who lives in a rural area told us about his family, "Yes, we always have been able to raise more corn per acre than our neighbors. It's a family secret." Because their behavior reflected upon their families, these youngsters had a strong moral sense of shame (shaming their families) and of "doing right" (bringing credit to their loved ones). One child said, "I wanted to make my grandparents proud of me because they are so sweet and worked so hard for all of us." This is an especially important finding in the light of the increasing alienation that exists between many youngsters and their families today.

These children easily absorbed their grandparents' attitudes, skills, and religious convictions. Because they were cared for, they, in their turn, cared for other family members. For them it was normal. They also enjoyed the relaxed and supportive relationship between their parents and their grandparents, and worried little when there were "normal miseries." They knew that the family fabric was strong and could support the daily stresses of life.

THE GRANDPARENTING INSTINCT

Grandparenting is not only "in the head," it is a deeply rooted emotional and behavioral instinct, a part of our biological nature. It is direct: genetically, grandparents and grandchildren are part of one another. Grandchildren carry one-fourth of each grandparent's genes, and often resemble their grandparents physically and may inherit their talents, temperaments, and even their foibles. They are part of one another.

Through the ages, grandparents and grandchildren have learned how to be together in their own unique way. After all, grandparents and grandchildren have spent their lives together over the past tens of thousands of years of recorded history while the middle generation ran the show. Even before the baby comes, grandparents undergo an unfolding of a profound psychological process that involves their thoughts, feelings, and behavior. This is reported by grandparents who, when a grandchild is born far away, experience a powerful urgent drive, as one grandparent told us, "to see the child and to feel it close to me, to hear its voice . . . to inspect it to see if everything is there . . . even to see a picture." This powerful urge to "see, hear, hold, and inspect" the new grandchild is understandable; biologists know that soon after a child (or an animal) is born, powerful instincts are activated within the parents and the child, instincts that determine whether the child will survive or not and that forge the powerful emotional bonds necessary for its survival. Grandparents are involved in this process: they report the urge to bond emotionally with the child as soon as it is born—to imprint the child in their mind—and to support the parents. This is an especially close moment for mothers and daughters.

The grandparenting instinct, our studies have shown, is expressed and fulfilled by the roles that grandparents play. These roles are an important part of the positive self-concept of the grandparent and indispensable for a happy relationship not only with their grandchildren, but with their own children.

GRANDPARENTS' ROLES

When a grandchild is born, a grandparent immediately becomes a *living ancestor* for the child and has the opportunity to emotionally bond to the new child and form a vital connection, a deep and enduring emotional attachment. At this time the new grandparent becomes a living historian for the child, a storehouse of information about other times and other places and how the family has lived and functioned through the passing years. Before the written word, grandparents were always the repository of information upon which the society relied. The new grandparent also becomes the chronicler of the living history of the child's parent. For children, only grandparents know the "real truth" about their parents. This enforces generational continuity. One gentleman that we met during our research maintained a "family museum" in his attic. His grandchildren happily foraged through love letters that their great-great-grandfather wrote to their great-great-grandmother and played with toys hundreds of years old. As mentors, grandparents teach children things that they learn nowhere else: ethics, morals, and behavior. One woman told us she became an attorney because her grandfather "who looked like Abraham Lincoln" taught her about "honesty and defending the innocent." Grandchildren learn from their grandparents in a non-pressured atmosphere of loving acceptance and unconditional love. "My grandparents don't give out report cards," one youngster told us. Family skills and secrets are often passed on by grandparents to grandchildren. A young woman who lives on Nantucket Island learned to make the family chowder from her grandfather. "He never taught me exactly how to make it. He just gave me the ingredients and told me to watch him. It took me two years to get it to taste the same, but I finally did it."

As nurturers grandparents are a natural safety net for the children when the parents falter. The nurturing role of grandparents is very important for parents, because they can find security in the knowledge that their parents are available to the family if adversity strikes. Childcare, nursing, counseling, caring for the children while the married couple spends needed time together, and providing financial and emotional support are only a few of the ways that grandparents can nurture their family.

In addition to those mentioned above, there are three other roles that are very special and become increasingly important as grandparents and grandchildren spend more time together: hero, wizard, and crony.

Age is fascinating to children. Wrinkles in a grandparent's face are a source of mystery. Seeing a grandparent remove a mouthful of teeth is a source of amazement to a young child. Baking bread out of flour and pulling fish from still ponds are sources of wonder when shared by an awed youngster and a patient grandparent. Grandparents can be heroic figures in children's humdrum lives in school or in front of the television screen. Where else could they hear from a man who worked in a Western coal mine and turned blue from the dust or who used to snap the heads off rattlesnakes before he cooked them? Imagine a grandmother who marched in parades "so that she would be allowed to vote." Grandparents are similar to the Wizard of Oz. For adults, they have no real powers, but they are magic in the eyes of their grandchildren. The fact that parents listen to grandparents is a source of incredulity to some children. Who else can, as one child told us, "boss my parents around?"

In the crony role, grandparents and grandchildren consort with one another against the powers that be—the middle generations—much to the chagrin of annoyed parents. One grandmother who owns a bar takes her young grandson inside and sits him up on the bar. "The customers love him," she told us, "but I try not to let his parents find out. We have a ball." A young woman told us that her grandfather let her drive his truck when she was eight years old but told her it was their "secret." The myth of grandparents spoiling grandchildren is rooted in the crony role. Parents are often envious that their own parents never treated them in this wonderfully carefree way. They feel left out of the fun. Mature parents understand this and, trusting their own parents, look the other way. But when parents are feuding with grandparents, crony behavior can aggravate family tensions. Recognizing the importance of the crony coalition, one cynic remarked, "Grandparents and grandchildren get along so well because they both have the same enemies."

Grandparents serve as role models for their grandchildren's attitudes, future old age, and future behavior as grandparents. Close and loving grandparents can be assured that their love and attention will be passed on to their great-grandchildren after they have died. And children with close grandparents extend their love and respect to other older people. This was graphically demonstrated to me while I was interviewing some very tough teenagers in a ghetto area in New York City. One street-hardened eighteen-year-old who had been convicted of several felonies told me, "I could take what I can from anyone I could except for the old people. They remind me of my grandmother. I tried to take an old lady's purse once but I felt sorry for her. It was like I was doing it to my grandmother. She was the only person who was good to me when I was a kid, and I didn't have to do anything for her. Only eat my food and go to school. It was when she died that I started getting into trouble. When she was alive I wouldn't do anything bad because I wanted her to be proud of me. I guess when she died, so did I."

THE NEW SOCIAL CONTRACT

Sadly, our original study showed that only fifteen percent of grandchildren had close grandparents and "vital connections." The rest faded in and out of their grandchildren's lives. What was happening to families? We have explained this in terms of the New Social Contract, an unstated agreement between parents and grandparents that has sheared apart many families. The contract is an agreement between parents and grandparents—most often, but not exclusively, mutual—that grandparents will no longer be involved in the rearing of their grandchildren.

In *Grandparents/Grandchildren* we explained: ". . . the evidence provided by such grandparents leads us to assert the existence of a powerful countervailing force which vitiates the instinct to grandparent and, with that instinct, the primordial bond between grandparents and grandchildren. This force is rooted in history, not biology, and is manifested by thoughts (and attitudes) rather than feelings. We call it 'the new social contract.' It is social because it is based on attitudes that have been learned and digested from family experience in a changing society. It is contractual because it assumes that parents can and should decide whether and to what extent grandparents will nurture their grandchildren. And it is new because it has developed within the lifespan of the current generation of grandparents." The terms of this contract involve not mutual support but mutual and complete independence, and the assurance of emotional isolation from one another.

During our research, we were surprised to find that a great degree of animosity exists between parents and grandparents. We will discuss this more fully in a later section. For the moment, however, suffice it to say that this arid emotional soil is not conducive to the growth of loving families.

What's special about the grandparent-grandchild bond is at the center of what life is about. Nature has made the bond second only in emotional power to the parent-child bond, benefiting not only the young and the old, but the parents, too. Nature has accorded special benefits to youngsters who have a vital connection to at least one grandparent, and designed the grandparent role as part of the emotional work of the elder. For the grandparent, it is no less than a reason for existence, a meaning for living.

The formidable task awaiting each new generation is to reap the benefits of what nature has given them. This is a challenge and an opportunity. The first thing is to learn to understand one another. This is no easy task, for even if parents and children have learned to understand each other very well, it all changes when a new baby comes along. All move one step up the generational ladder. Children become parents and parents become grandparents. They are enhanced, but they also must come to learn about one another all over again.

THREE

Up the Generational Ladder

The first child born into a family shifts the status of parents and children permanently into another generation, and their relationship takes on an added dimension. For the first time parents tread the same road as their own parents and begin to view their own parents differently: "Maybe they knew more than I thought they did," said one new mother. Parents who were intent on "doing their own thing" before the baby came now need the expertise of grandparents who have weathered the trials and tribulations of raising kids. After all, new parents are living evidence that their own parents know how to do it.

A good parent-child and in-law relationship opens the door to a healthy three-generational system. A problem-ridden grandparent–in-law relationship can doom the three-generational system from the start and permanently separate grandparents from grandchildren. New parents who are immature or feuding with the new grandparents are fearful that their parents will "damage" their child in the same way that they perceive themselves as damaged, and so they wish to "protect" their child from grandparents.

Mature parents are self-confident; they will have devoted sufficient time to learning about themselves and fulfilling some of their personal dreams and goals before devoting their life to a child.

Young marrieds need a period of time together to become profoundly familiar with each other before they add a baby to their family. Whatever joys the baby will bring, it will also take time that parents might well use to be with each other. Grandparents can use a time-out between the rearing of their own children (which never ends—parenting, for better or worse, is a lifelong process) and taking on the grandparent role. It's a rest that is in order and well deserved.

When these conditions aren't met, difficulties arise. Everyday conflicts can explode into major problems. An immature mother, for example, may expect her parents to raise her child, thus relegating herself to the role of an older sister. All she has done is add another child to the family. When this happens, the family structure remains functionally two-generational even though three biological generations are present. New roles have not been assumed. Grandparents remain parents. Their child, the erstwhile parent, remains a child . . . but with a baby. When the normal chronological system is short-circuited, trouble can start. (We will talk more about this in a later section.)

The kind of family that a new baby joins has a profound effect on the quality of life for the child. The nature and personality of families are diverse and formed by a consensus of their members. Thus families come in all shapes and forms, serving the needs of their members in infinite ways. For babies, parents, and grandparents there are good and not-so-good families. The best is what I call the natural family system, an ideal human arrangement that provides for the happiness and support of all its members. Although difficult to attain for most of us, it is an example to emulate, in whole or in part, as closely as possible.

AN IDEAL FAMILY SYSTEM

The natural family is comprised of people who are rooted in the past, live in the present, and consider and plan for the future. Although it's hard to believe in today's times, such people really exist.

I call this system "natural" because it is a basic way in which human beings following their biological order can relate to and nurture and support one another. It is primitive in the sense that it is basic. Such a family serves the emotional needs of its members and offers a safety net for life support. Most of the typical "natural" families that I met during my research lived close to one another, and several families were involved in farming or in a family business together. The system benefits even friends and relatives who are fortunate enough to be included. The natural system offers a very positive model for each new generation. It is a total family culture.

If the following description appears sentimental and idealized, it is because the natural family is based on an affectionate emotional attachment and a spiritual philosophy. It's an important part of the way its members are. It may be difficult for some people to read the following description of the natural family without becoming irritated or sad when they contrast it with their own state of affairs. This is understandable; current attitudes, mobility, and economic pressures mitigate against natural families. Who wouldn't prefer to live in a natural family? But there are lessons to be learned here so that people can improve their own varied situations.

Members of the natural family have as many foibles, feuds, and eccentricities as anyone else, but what is most impressive is their ability to maintain their close emotional bonds and family unity under the most adverse circumstances. They stick together. Below are some of the attributes of the natural family.

FAMILY RELATIONSHIPS

The family interactions are intergenerational. All family members spend time with one another and sometimes work together. Childcare is shared by all generations. Family members have well-defined roles. Although their roles may shift back and forth, they don't invade one another's territory. A grandmother, for example, may take over a parenting role in the parents' absence when requested, but will return to being a supportive grandmother when the parents return. Family members talk to one another. Communication is direct. Each family member's self-image is dependent on family standing and not on material wealth or social status. John, a blacksmith in a small New England town, is highly respected by his family. His mother describes him affectionately: "I have a son who makes a lot of money in New York but he is not half the son that John is." For John, his family is "the reason for living." "I know I don't make a good living, but I also know that there are more important things in life than that. I am loved and needed and important in my family. The people that I care about love me—that's what counts for me."

Just as love and loyalty are deeply felt, so is anger. When family feuds occur, the sparks fly. But members of natural families usually work things out. They are not emotionally cut off from one another because they are linked through some group that acts as peacemaker and arbiter. "I am the family peacemaker," Nana, a California grandmother, told us. "I have twelve grandchildren and six kids and they are constantly at one another. This husband hates this brother-in-law . . . it goes on and on. I get in there and straighten it all out. They really don't mind me butting in, either. Sometimes they back themselves into a corner with their big mouths. Someone has got to bail them out." When adversity strikes, the family turns to its members for help before it turns to social institutions or "paid strangers."

CHILDREN AND PARENTS

Children raised in a natural family setting are in an emotional paradise. They feel important because they *are* important. Children have what they want and need most: many people who are crazy about them and available to them if their parents aren't able to care for them. They like and respect people and are very social. They respect the family system and look forward to continuing their own family someday. They are allowed to remain children—no one is in a hurry for them to grow up—yet at the same time they contribute (as best they can considering they are children) to the family by doing their chores or jobs. There are no "latchkey kids" in this group. Someone is always there for them.

Living among a natural family makes marriage and parenthood easier. When the pressures of parenthood overwhelm a young couple, the spillover can be easily absorbed by a supportive family. "It's so helpful to us, my husband and me, to have the family so happy when we go off. They just can't wait to have our kids," one mother told me. Married people cannot supply everything for each other. The natural family supplies enough people so that the marriage does not implode, two people trying to impossibly be all things to one another. One father said, "I am so glad that Alice, my wife, has her mother and sisters to talk to. There's stuff that I can't help her with. She needs her family. I can't be her mother and sister and girlfriend, too. Sure, I am her best friend, but married people aren't supposed to supply it all for one another; it isn't human. With her family around, we're all happier."

GRANDPARENTS AND GREAT-GRANDPARENTS

Grandparents are the natural family's emotional leaders and define the philosophy by which it lives. It is through the family that elders share the wisdom and experience that they have accumulated through the years. The older the person, the more respect he or she has in the family. They contribute to the family personality. They are given an important ceremonial role in family functions and celebrations. A young man told me that his ninety-six-year-old great-grandfather "stands as the head of the family. He doesn't do much, but he doesn't have to. All he has to do is to be there."

Children usually adore their elders: "My grandmother is old, but look at all the family she has. Can you imagine all she did to bring all these people along? She is so cute and everyone is crazy about her. I want to be like her. She raised all these [eight] children and ran a grocery store. Wonder woman, that's my grandmother."

"My family, that is what I do," said her grandmother.

BONDS NOT BONDAGE

Nothing is perfect. Some adolescents within natural families view the closeness and caring of the family as "stifling" and tradition as being "out of it." The family is slow to absorb social change, and family members may be regarded by youngsters as too traditional—"fuddy-duddy," as one told me. Ethnic traditions, languages, and "old ways" are preserved. The family culture is respected by the group. Their main unifying forces are the family personality (family members speak of themselves as "we"), being geographically near to one another (a critical factor), and spending time with one another. These factors—time, place, and undivided attention to one another—are the basic ingredients of the vital connection. These factors can make for deep emotional attachments between people. Emotional bonds are not viewed as emotional bondage. Adversity is more easily absorbed. New members by adoption or remarriage and family friends are included automatically.

The natural family system works because of an unspoken contract between its members that they will be committed to one another, share common values, be supportive of one another, and act as part of a cohesive unit. The elder members of the family have shown the way; they demonstrate the value of this family philosophy. The family has an emotional leader. The leader is usually chosen by the elders in an unspoken decision. Jason, a farmer in Appalachia, is a natural grandfather and the leader of his family. He already knew who would be next and would "watch out for the family" after him. One afternoon, as we were standing on the front porch of his farm on a hot summer's day looking out over his fields, his young grandaughter Sarah was cavorting on the grass in front of us with her new puppy, Perry. "She's next when her mother passes on," said Jason. "She'll be the heart of our family, just like her mother, just like her grandmother and Elsa, her great-grandmother. She's got what it takes." (I will discuss in a later chapter the special qualities of altruism and family consciousness that Jason knows about and feels instinctively.) These are the special qualities that he has spotted in Sarah and are the stuff of which "real" grandparents are made.

The natural family is comprised of people with different temperaments, characters, interests, and talents, but the family tries to respect these differences and the individuality of its members. Family members relate to one another in diverse ways, according to an emotional protocol dictated by their biological relationship—parent, grandparent, uncle, etc. This in turn gives them a sense of place and order. One youngster described this pecking order: "Uncle John can't boss me around like my father or mother can. He can take me places and give me ideas, but he can't punish me. He hasn't the right like my parents or grandparents have."

What are the rights of parents and grandparents within the family? We can learn this by examining how the relationship works and how it evolves over time.

FOUR

Parents, Grandparents, and Kids: How They Relate

Grandparents, parents, and kids relate to one another in totally different ways. Keep in mind that although a kid's relationship to his or her parents and grandparents is direct, the relationship between a grandparent and parent is double-edged: each party is both parent and child.

PARENTS AND CHILDREN

The child grows within and is born from the mother's body. It is genetically half its father and half its mother; parents and children are part of one another. For a child the relationship is mandatory: without parents the child will die. For parents it is obligatory: they are responsible for the welfare of the child not only biologically (instinctively), but also in the eyes of society (they *have* to). To some parents this may seem a burden. It is a permanent relationship; they will always be parent and child. They live in different historic times, and thus the relationship is intergenerational.

Parents have an authoritative position vis-à-vis the child. They determine nearly all the aspects of the child's existence, from the regulation of bodily functions to the way the child will dress, speak, and live. Parents and children have no choice in these matters. They are stuck with each another.

The relationship changes throughout the years. The child becomes more self-determined and independent. The parents' responsibility for the child decreases, and parental authority wanes. Parental obligations decrease over the years. The burden, if present, lessens.

Affection between parents and children is a complex issue. There are two components. The first is unconditional love and loyalty, a natural bond between parents and their progeny. The second, more complicated, is a conditional system—love given for performance, for meeting the needs and demands of another. Parents naturally view their children as projections of themselves and their hope for realizing their secret dreams. Thus, at the extreme, a child could be only an instrument, a projection of a parent (i.e., the classic stereotype of the "stage mother"). Conditional love is given when the child pleases the parent and withdrawn when the child transgresses the boundaries determined by the parent. "Good" children are adored. "Bad" children are punished. Parents take their children's performance very personally. Parents with children who have problems, no matter what the reason, often think that they have "failed," while a "good" child can make a star out of his or her parents.

Conditional love places an emotional burden on children. They know that whatever they do, their parents are affected. Thus they naturally want to separate from this system, to be liberated from the emotional bondage of "guilt trips" from their parents. Often they seek to establish a unique identity, a sense of their own history and their own community. They form their identity using the parent's identity as something to bounce off, something to be unlike, something to be different from.

All human relationships can be discussed and examined using these factors as a framework. For example, we find them at work in the sibling relationship. Siblings share the same genes. They are permanently related to one another. They live in a staggered sequence of historical time. They may or may not share the same chronological world. Their relationship is commonly intragenerational. Affection is surely there, but is colored by competition. Brothers and sisters battle one another to be the favorite in the eyes of their parents. They are especially attuned to one another's faults and flaws, and they are quick to broadcast them publicly. They are usually not responsible for one another and do not have an authoritative role toward one another (older children are often the exception). They do like to establish their own turf, to be different. (This is especially obvious in the case of twins.) They are not a burden to one another.

Sibling relationships evolve and change over the years. Their affection for one another is both conditional and unconditional: "I can hate my brother's guts in the morning and play with him in the evening," said Jill, a twelve-year-old, demonstrating the often tempestuous nature of the sibling bond. Is this perhaps the way that nature teaches children how to have a knock-down drag-out fight, to practice their assertiveness, while building their emotional tolerance so as not to emotionally isolate themselves from one another? There is a lot to learn by observing children fight with one another —if a parent can stand the heat.

GRANDPARENTS AND GRANDCHILDREN

The grandparent-grandchild bond is biological and genetic. Grandchildren carry one-fourth of a grandparent's genes. It is permanent and an intergenerational relationship. Grandparents and grandchildren live in both the same and different historical time, and they have something in common: a complex relationship with the middle generation, the parents. Grandparents are responsible for their grandchildren not only directly but indirectly by their responsibility for their own children, responsibility once removed and extended into another generation. The relationship is not mandatory, because neither party is responsible for the other's physical welfare—that's the parents' job. For the most part they are not a burden to each other. It is this factor—the absence of burden—that contributes mightily to the positive aspects of the grandparent-grandchild bond. One woman put it well: "My kids were a lot to handle sometimes. I could never get away, even for a moment. I can have a great time with my grandchildren, but I am not on duty for twenty-four hours a day, seven days a week. I'm up when I am with them."

Since grandparents are not usually directly responsible for grandchildren, their egos are not as mixed up with them. Thus their affectionate bonds lack the conditionality of the parent-child love bond. Grandparents love grandchildren because they breathe. Jean-Paul Sartre said that he could drive his grandmother into raptures of joy just by being hungry. That's what unconditional love is all about. Grandparents have a limited and varied amount of authority over grandchildren, but children naturally respect age, so grandparental authority is benevolent and not punitive. Few children try to "get away" with things when their grandparents are involved (unless they have an unusually authoritative grandparent).

Because children usually do not have to use their grandparents to form their own identity, grandparents can offer a permanent and unchanging sanctuary for children. Jimmy, seventeen years old, said, "I go to my grandparents whenever I fight with my parents. They haven't changed over the years like my parents have. They are always kind and understanding. I can always go to my grandfather's store when I'm hassling with my parents or sleep over at their house whenever I want to." Grandparents' roles are diverse yet permanent.

Children will view and use their grandparents in different ways at different times. For young children, grandparents are primarily caretakers, wizards, historians, and heroes. For teenagers they are ancestors, historians, family counselors, and cronies. For adults they are historians, nurturers, cronies, and role models. All these roles are there for the taking at whatever age the child has need of them. The relationship changes as the grandparent and child grow older, but within a fixed system; it's never really different. Their relationship doesn't evolve toward separation as an adolescent and reunion as an adult, as does a healthy parent-child relationship.

What the child does see is the grandparent grow old. Perhaps the child encounters death for the first time through the demise of the grandparent. When young children lose a grandparent, the grandparent never grows old in the child's mind and is embedded in the mind and heart of the child permanently. Most often these are fond and powerful memories that influence the life decisions and attitudes of the child. A young mother told me, "I was not allowed to mourn when my grandmother died. No one realized what I was going through. The adults had the public mourning. I had the private one. She died when I was eight years old. I still talk to her when I am alone, and I have taught my children about her. I never could tell the adults what I felt. They never knew. She is a part of me today. How I am as a mother and how I will be as a grandmother, that's my secret with Gammy."

Grandparents often have a magic ingredient that harried parents do not: time. And, in the best of circumstances, they also have a non-pressured atmosphere in which to share that time. Men, especially, have time available as grandfathers that they never had as fathers. While this can often lead to rivalry between parents and children for the time and attention of the parent/grandfather, it is a priceless gift to the kids.

Although children are acutely aware of their parents' likes and dislikes—sometimes the better to disagree with them and thus be different—they have no deep-seated psychological urge to be unlike their grandparents. They may not agree with some grandparental views, but the negative fuel and vehement unrest—the "chronic emergency"[1] so evident in most adolescents—is usually not present in their dealings with their grandparents. Most children are naturally sweet to devoted grandparents because nature has not built in any tensions between them, in contrast to the evident tensions that are an integral part of the way that parents and children relate. Thus it is especially important that grandparents remain constant for

1. David L. Gutman, "Deculturation and the American Grandparent," *Grandparenthood.* Bengston & Robertson, eds. Beverly Hills: Sage Press, 1984, pp. 181–182.

children when the parents are having problems. Children never have to leave their grandparents. The relationship should have enough resiliency and roles for grandparents so that it can absorb anything that life can throw at it—as do healthy parent-child relationships.

WHEN GRANDCHILDREN COME ALONG

When a new grandchild arrives on the scene, an important emotional shift occurs. A powerful bonding takes place between generations. Powerful feelings are unleashed between the new parents and grandparents. A young mother from a close family spoke about her feelings soon after she gave birth: "It was more than a private thing between Al [her husband] and me. When I gave birth, that baby brought me so close to my mother. Something magic happened. The way Mom held my hand and touched me. I was never so close to her. And my father—he was so happy. I feel that I gave him something that he couldn't do for himself. That I finally reached him. I think, secretly, the baby was a special gift for my father, and for me. But it really was for everyone. You see, when I gave birth I really accomplished something."

The first days of the new family are crucial. Diplomatic grandparents are needed to teach and to nurture the young parents so that they can have time for the new child. But wise grandparents do not usurp the authority of the new parents. Sometimes overenthusiastic grandparents, blinded by their enthusiasm for the new baby, forget whose child it is and threaten the authority and newfound territory of the new parent. Grandmothers can be the most frequent offenders. Most grandfathers are a bit shy with new babies and don't get in the way too much, at least not at this time. The early days are usually the time of the grandmother. Wise grandparents know that most young parents are insecure and frightfully unsure of themselves (some lose sleep at night listening intently to hear if their newborn is still breathing), and realize that their own parent-child relationship has been altered permanently. How grandparents respond to this event will ultimately determine the quality of the relationship that they will have with their children and, via them, their grandchildren. This is a critical time.

Mature young parents do not feel threatened or inadequate when asking the "experts," their own parents, for advice. They do not resent having to do so. However, it may make an immature parent feel inadequate, for fear of reverting to the role of a child. But nature routinely places new parents, especially mothers, in a dependent "childlike" role temporarily. This is understandable. Mothers need someone to take care of them. Sensitive grandparents can do this without making their child feel ignorant or inadequate. Insensitive grandparents, unfortunately not recognizing the temporary regression taking place in their formerly "grown-up" child, often ignore the panic new parents experience, their disorientation and confusion with their new role. They may respond in a critical, impatient, or negative manner and relegate the young parent to the role of an ignorant child. Trouble starts. The parent fears that he or she has relinquished newly-found autononomy and has given the parents back the mantle of authority that the young parent has been rebelling against most of his or her life. When this happens—and it is not uncommon—grandparents keep their child from assuming their rightful parental role. Grandparents who do this reverse their roles and squelch not only the parenthood of their children but deny themselves the function of grandparent. They become, in effect, older parents. In such a situation a new parent will react in the only way possible, by running away from the oppressive grandparents. Grandparents who are not sensitive at this stage will often lose not only their children but their grandchildren as well. This all too common scenario can herald the premature end of the three-generational family.

During the first days after the birth of a child, the new family must be on the alert for other potential difficulties. Parents may get jealous of the grandparents' attention to the new baby, especially if one of the parents was shortchanged in this department by his or her own parents. Competition between grandparents and parents for the baby's affection is not uncommon. These and other situations may become exaggerated to the point where parents view grandparents more as a liability than an asset and limit the grandparents' visits. It is then, during the first days of the new family, that nature gives both parents and children an opportunity to do it over again —a regeneration.

Mark, a young father, learned this well: "I never got along with my parents. I ran away from home several times. I got into trouble with the police for drinking, and I even robbed a few houses when I was doing drugs. As you see, I have straightened out. But I always felt guilty about hurting my parents, who are nice people. When I got married, they couldn't believe I got such a nice girl, and then when my little son came along, I found that I could make them happy. My boy has made an enormous difference between my parents and myself. I can laugh with them. I feel like I did a good thing and I brought them joy. My son has made it up to them. My folks always wanted to be grandparents. I made them that way. I made them grandparents." Mark's parents took the opportunity of becoming involved and loving grandparents with their new grandchild and started over. Mark's father said: "It was a new beginning with me and Mark with the child. He began to understand me. After all, we both are fathers. We have something in common."

Becoming grandparents offered Mark's parents the opportunity to reunite their family. There are grandparents who, like Mark's parents, await this opportunity, and others who don't care at all. How does this happen?

FIVE

What Makes a Grandparent?

People who take their grandparenting seriously are like devoted parents; they are born that way. I call them "naturals." Jason, in chapter 2, described his grandaughter Sarah in this way. She instinctively, in his words, "has what it takes." Sarah is a natural. I like the term because it describes the qualities of a person who is the emotional heart and physical center of a family. A natural is "tuned in" emotionally and intuitively to the emotional aspects of situations, has an abundance of common sense, knows things that aren't taught in schools, and feels his or her way through life. People with this gift place an emotional priority on their lives, attract other people to them, and are beloved by many people. They usually are well known in their communities. Naturals make wonderful grandparents. The ones I met during my research taught me a great deal about the ingredients of a real grandparent. They feel the appropriate way to act with other people. They are excellent parents, and thus have prepared themselves to be involved grandparents because their children want them to do so. They possess the most important characteristic of the grandparent: natural altruism. If the other factors that influence the quality of grandparenting—vitality, readiness, a satisfying life experience as a grandchild, and having their own parents involved with their own children—are present, they are largely immune from negative cultural attitudes toward grandparenting. Nothing short of not having a family can stop them from being involved grandparents.

Obviously, people who are not endowed with natural altruism can be effective grandparents too, but it's just not as easy to attain the degree of closeness, family involvement, and esteem that a natural does. All of us have this gift in some degree. Even people with only minimal natural interest in others can be involved grandparents if they develop the interest, have the vitality, and have had a positive role model for grandparenting. They can act out of learned example for the benefit of their children and grandchildren.

The following factors are important not only for grandparents to strive for, but also for parents as well.

ALTRUISM

In the dictionary, altruism is defined as "unselfish concern for the welfare of others." Altruistic people, in my view, are just born that way. They demonstrate their altruistic nature throughout their lives, as the compassionate child who cries when a loved one is injured, the caring and charitable adult helping the less fortunate, or the involved and devoted elder ministering to family and community. It is not gender-linked. Men and women can be equally altrusitic. Infant studies show that certain infants will "mirror" other people's distress—they are responsive to pain in others. Other infants, on the other hand, react little or not at all. This is what altruistic behavior is all about. Like all emotions, it's hard to prove—it can only be witnessed or felt.

One grandfather explains his own altruistic views:

> I don't ever want to hurt another human being, and that is my life philosophy. Knowing that, I know how to behave in most situations. I think of how my actions will affect people before I do things. I think of how my children would feel about what I was doing and if my act would be hurtful. I guess I get

> guilty easily. It's not a fear of God or punishment that stops me . . . it's just me. I don't want to hurt anyone. Being kind makes me happy. I don't know where that comes from. I am not religious, although I respect other people's religion. . . .

People may do altruistic and caring acts but differ in motivation, although not behavior, from natural altruism. Another grandfather, Mr. Markel, behaves altruistically although he would "rather be golfing":

> Sometimes it's a pain to visit the kids at the hospital with the men's group at my church. I don't enjoy it too much although I know that the kids do. I do it because it's part of my religious life. When the day comes that I am at the pearly gates and they look at the ledger book, this will be one good mark for me. Personally, I'd rather be golfing.

A well-known geneticist, Edward O. Wilson, stated that "altruistic genes assure their preservation."[2] Devoted grandparents seem to act on that premise, guarding and protecting their families. A grandmother who came to America from Sicily in 1920 did that automatically. "The most important thing that I learned from my own grandfather is that children need protection, guidance, and discipline. Each child is a sacred trust. They should be under the watchful eye of a relative until they grow up. When a member of my family is hurting, I actually feel it."

Unfortunately, modern society does not foster altruistic behavior. Even people who have a bent toward acting altruistically may find it hard to do so today because their families aren't near them or are too busy to have time for them. I have spoken with altruistic parents who bemoaned the fact that their disinterested parents were too "self-centered" to be involved with them and their children. Altruistic grandparents and grandchildren suffer when they are de-

---

2. Edward O. Wilson, *On Human Nature.* Cambridge, Mass.: Harvard University Press, 1978, p. 159.

prived of each other's company by a disinterested middle generation.

I asked a young grandmother why she was able to nurture not only her family but her neighbor's children, serve on the school board, be active in church activities, and still be available to help whenever she was needed, even in the middle of the night when she rode the ambulance. "I guess I am just a nice person. I don't know why. I'm sure not like Ann down the street. She was a lousy kid, a conceited teenager, a rotten parent, and a conceited old biddy. She doesn't have a decent bone in her body. I am not like that, I am naturally good-natured. I care about others."

VITALITY

Another important factor is vitality. Fortunately, the new generation of grandparents, healthier than any generation of grandparents before them, will be more vital than ever, the better to do the work cut out for them. This is an important personality characteristic. Vital people brighten the world for everyone. The ability to be a broad-spectrum grandparent—to integrate family responsibilities, work, and personal growth—depends upon the degree of health and vigor of the individual. Understandably, mental and physical health and life situation play an important part in determining vitality.

Patty, eight years old, described her vital grandparent for us:

> She is a dynamo. A speedball. She comes over on Sunday morning with a bag all full of stuff. She is amazing. She can dance up a storm, and I get tired before she does. When my Mom was sick in the hospital she came over and cleaned the house and did the cooking. Of course I helped her; we did it together. I never saw such pep before. She could run my mother and father into the ground. She even chops wood. Would you believe that she is sixty-seven years old . . . sixty-seven . . . hope I am like that. She says that I am.

Like altruism, some individuals are gifted with great vitality, a strong life force. But unlike altruism, vitality doesn't necessarily affect the quality of grandparenting, just the quantity. John, one grandfather we met in Nebraska, was described by his wife as a "pretty lazy guy who sits out in the shed all day carving out shingles." Although John isn't physically active, he is certainly doing something right because he constantly has children begging him to teach them how to carve wood figures and make birchbark birdhouses. "I like the peace and quiet," he told me. "I don't like fuss and noise. The kids and grands know this. They can come out here anytime that they want but they can't make no noise." His "grands" told me that Grandpa John "didn't move around too much. It's a family joke about having to move him if a fire ever broke out. But if you listen to him carefully he's a very funny person. Just quiet. The opposite of Grandma."

THE RIGHT TIME—"READINESS"

There is a right time to become a grandparent. Age isn't the major indicator, although some say that the best time is between forty-five and sixty years of age. Readiness has to do primarily with life situation. Ideally, new parents will have grown up, established their own households, and attained financial autonomy, allowing their own parents a rest. During this respite grandparents are off duty and free from child care. It is a time for them to re-evaluate their own lives and to realign their priorities. After this period of respite, people have told me that they are ready to become grandparents. Some "can't wait," especially altruistic and family-oriented grandparents. One grandmother who was ready was "getting bored. I need kids around and I am angry at my kids for not giving us grandchildren. What's the big deal about their 'career'? Kids are what's important." This pressure to produce grandchildren is also felt by the middle generation. A young husband feels "guilty that I am not having a kid. That's all my parents talk about: when is the baby coming? That's what I hear when I am around them. Aren't I good enough, or did they bring me into the world to deliver them a grandchild?"

If a person isn't ready, grandparenthood can be unwelcome. "I'm just not ready," a thirty-five-year-old grandmother from New York told me. "My kids are just about grown up and my daughter shacks up with this guy and has a baby. We don't believe in abortion. I have a job, too. Who is going to watch this kid? I was looking forward to a rest." Her problem extended into another generation: "My mother is a great-grandmother and she is only sixty. Everything is mixed up. I feel like the new baby's mother and my daughter like a sister. I tell you that I am not ready for all this. My husband and I need a little time together, we have a hard life. Of course the baby will be well cared for, but I wish my daughter could have waited ten years. Then it would have been fun to have a new baby around and I could be a real grandmother, like the storybooks, like the one that I had. I'm worried that I am going to miss out on that, maybe when I am a great-grandmother."

Grandparents deserve some time to get their second wind. If they are not given this, it may affect another important determinant of an individual's ability to grandparent: an individual's availability.

AVAILABILITY

The new generation will have difficulty being available to grandparent. Not only do many families no longer live near one another, increasing long-distance grandparenting or "telegrandparenting," but many grandparents are working longer than ever before.[3] Increasingly women, potential full-time grandmothers, are entering the work force. Growing numbers of grandparents are retiring far away from their families. Issues such as divorce, remarriage, the death of a spouse, health, and many others complicate things even further. The pain caused by the unavailability of grandparents is felt

3. In a conversation with Dr. Stanley A. Cath at a meeting of the Boston Gerontological Society in 1984.

not only by grandchildren, who do not see otherwise loving and devoted grandparents enough, but by parents.

One mother, Julie, had made an effort to move near her parents to have a "whole family" and was upset because her mother got a full-time job. "I don't know why she did that. I went to so much trouble to move back home. My husband even took a cut in pay. My mom went out to work and now she has no time for us. And when she does, she's tired." Her mother realizes this and plans to do something about it: "I want to be near the kids and be involved. I am just so happy working. I never worked out of the house before and I am getting a kick out of it. I guess I'll cut back on my hours so I can spend more time with the kids. It might be the best of both worlds." Julie's mother all by herself discovered the secret of being a worker and an available grandparent: flexibility in her work schedule and balance in prioritizing her time between work and family. Most grandparents have some control over their availability and can do the same.

PERSONAL EXPERIENCE

The degree of exposure that people have had to grandparenting greatly influences their attitudes and behavior toward grandparenting. This happens in at least three ways: how one was treated as a grandchild, how his or her own grandparents behaved toward their children, and the effect of prevailing social attitudes.

Paul, thirty-two, is the father of three:

> I know what I am doing with my family and where I am going. I am copying what my grandfather did. He was a wonderful friend to me. I learned so much from him. I had a bit of hassle with my dad, and he always got us together. Now I see my own father doing the same things for my kids, getting them out of hot water with me. I'll probably do the same for my grandkids. I think I would resent my father interfering if

> my grandfather hadn't done the same thing on my behalf. Now I think it's kind of nice . . . sort of a game.
>
> I guess my grandfather taught me how to be a grandfather without me ever knowing it.

Many grandparents do not have positive role models and yet have become "real" grandparents. Mrs. Hillberg, a grandmother who is very involved with her family, said that her father left Europe when she was three and she never saw her grandparents again. They were killed in the war. "I adopted an older aunt as a 'grandma.' She was wonderful to me. My mother died when I was only nine, but my father and I stayed close. He was a wonderful grandfather to my children. Maybe that's where I get it from. Or maybe it's just me."

People who grandparent their own and other's grandchildren without having had a grandparent of their own are not rare. Mr. Reilly, seventy-five, works in a neighborhood day-care center his own grandchildren attend. He claims that he "wasn't fortunate enough to have had a grandparent of my own, being an orphan, but it sure doesn't stop me from being a good one."

Although experiential factors are important to grandparenting, the lack of them is no roadblock to altruistic people. They will become "real" parents and grandparents anyway. These factors do have a strong influence upon people who are not naturals. Since non-naturals are hard put to grandparent instinctively, they need social approval for their behavior and strong role models to imitate. The lack of these models can hamper their grandparenting unless they are lucky enough to have a grandchild that will bully it out of them. Mr. Robinson, a banker from the Midwest, has such a grandaughter:

> She's crazy about me. She gets excited when I am around. She calls me up and can't wait to see me. Frankly, I am not too interested in kids. I find them boring. I never had many adults in my life. I was raised in a foster home because my parents died in a fire when I was young and I didn't have any family interested enough in me to raise me. I was always a loner, lost in books and work until I met my wife. My little Mimi, my grandaughter, won't let me be a loner. She can't get enough of

> me. The funny thing is, she's got to me pretty good. The older she gets, the more I enjoy her. Next week I am taking her to the zoo. Funny, I never went to the zoo before. Maybe I am taking the kid in me to the zoo too. Maybe she's helping me make up for all that I missed. Hmmm.

Mr. Robinson has found, through his grandaughter, the young deprived child within himself. He is learning how to be a grandparent by virtue of Mimi's lessons and his natural attraction to her. This powerful force overcomes his reluctance to become involved. Mimi is his only teacher in the art of grandparenting, but a good one. He is fortunate, since, like many of his contemporaries, he did not learn its importance from his society.

WHAT SOCIETY SAYS ABOUT GRANDPARENTING

Prevailing social attitudes and behavior toward grandparenting have a profound effect upon the way that an individual views the role. If the society honors the role—as in Japan, where grandmothers may wear the color red as a badge of grandparenthood, or in some African communities, where grandparents are given the honored title "Noble"—people look forward to becoming grandparents with pride and joy. However, in much of the industrialized world, there is no recognized and accepted social celebration of becoming a grandparent. The growth and cultivation of emotional attachments that are the domain and the expertise of grandparents is far from being viewed as a priority issue in contemporary society. And so one of the most important challenges of the new generations is to examine how prevailing social attitudes have affected their own attitudes and behavior. This done, it is incumbent upon them, like Mr. Robinson, to call upon the positive forces nature has built in: their altruism, love for their families, the love of their families, dedication, and ingenuity to neutralize the negative effects of their personal and social experience impeding their vital connections.

GRANDFATHER AND I

by Joseph Concha

Grandfather and I
talk
Grandfather sings
I dance
Grandfather teaches
I learn
Grandfather dies
I cry

I wait
patiently
to see Grandfather
in the world of darkness

I miss
my
Grandfather

Patient waiting
is weighted
by loneliness
I cry and cry and cry
When
will I see him?

SIX

Grandfathers—From Warrior to Wise Man

Nature primes older men for becoming grandfathers. As men age, hormonal changes mellow them; they usually become more patient, reflective, and contemplative. These newfound qualities are ideal for dealing with children. If older men are interested in their families and find the time to spend with them, they have the opportunity, perhaps for the first time in their lives, to nurture and to enjoy their children and grandchildren.

Often men do not understand the value of these changes. They may view the diminution of their physical energy and sexual and competitive drives only as a lessening of their power, and ignore its advantages: the enhanced ability to be closer to people and to the emotional side of life. This is because many of today's middle-aged men were not taught to "be" with people.

Today's grandfathers were raised when men were taught to be tough and to show little emotion. "Men don't cry" was the watchword. Their job was to provide. "Real men" worked, primarily away from their families. They often lived in the work world, palled around with their male colleagues, and functioned in a competitive and adversarial environment. In effect, they lived as warriors, in the "macho" ethic. Their women held down the fort. Emotions, close relationships, and the kids came with the fort, and in many cases the men were left out of life within the family. Work is all they had.

Thus "mellowing out" can be frightening to men who can't shift gears when they get older. They must leave the warrior behind them, and celebrate what they have received in its place, wisdom and experience, the qualities of a master teacher.

WHAT AGE DOES TO MEN

Daddy Wells, a seventy-year-old grandfather, explained this process to me one afternoon while his family listened intently. He lives on a small farm in Texas "where men are men and women like it," he says jokingly. He describes himself as "a hard man" in his younger days. His son, Harold, calls him "strong and confident, a good father providing for his family," in those days. Mr. Wells agreed. "I was a hard-ass in those days; I didn't know it then but I know it now." He said that he couldn't cry in front of the family, for "that would be weakness. I couldn't show my feelings, especially at work. The men would've laughed me out of the drilling business. In those days the harder a man was, the more respect he got." "He was so hard," his son continued, "that we all avoided him like the plague. He was harsh and critical."

"That's true," said Mr. Wells. "I didn't have such fun at home then. I used to go out with the boys for a good time." Ann, his oldest daughter, remembered that during the Depression, "My respect for Dad grew. He worked day and night to put food on the table. He held three jobs. I never saw him much, but I knew that he was working for all of us." "Never took from the welfare, either," said Mr. Wells; "would've lost my self-respect."

"He changed completely when he became a grandfather," said Harold, smiling at his father. His younger daughter, Alice, a physician, chimed in, "He is more patient now. He sits and talks with us. Before he was always going somewhere or doing something. This is the first chance that I have to really get to know him." She laughed. "He is a captive audience. I can move faster than him now. Boy, his grandchildren have it made. He is wonderful with them, and I am not embarrassed to say that I am a bit jealous of my own kids and the fun they have with Dad."

Mr. Wells is aware that he has changed now that he has no public image to uphold:

> I cried publicly for the first time in my life when my granddaughter gave the valedictorian talk at the high school graduation. In the past I couldn't have done that. Well, since I've gotten older I don't care about appearances anymore. I know that I am a man no matter what I do. I was more insecure when I was younger. I used to punish the boys [his children] when they cried. I let the girls alone about that—that's for girls, I thought. I am so different with my grandchildren. They can do what they like and cry all they want. I never punish them for anything. I can cry and laugh with them like I never did with my own kids. Becoming a grandfather made me grow up. I feel sorry that I never treated my own kids with the patience and understanding that I have for my grandchildren.

Age has not emasculated Mr. Wells. Rather, he has surpassed himself and become a broader, more accepting person. He has made the transition from warrior to wise man. This is a natural transition, available to all men.

RELINQUISHING THE COMPETITIVE WAY

Whether they want to or not, older men are forced to relinquish the physical and competitive manner in which they were taught to deal with the world. They have two options: to drop out of life as they continue what they are doing and eventually burn out and are surpassed by the younger colleagues who are lusting after their position and status; or, to graduate into a new stage of life, become a "wise man," and use the gift of wisdom and experience in their relationships.

Mr. Bittle uses his brains instead of brawn:

> I sure ain't as frisky as I used to be, but when it comes to usin' the noggin' to buy right, there is no one here that can spot a winner better than me. I see the bad 'uns [cattle] that the young guys buy. I help them, if they ask nice. I can't ride my horse anymore but I've traded that to become the best cattle buyer around.

Although Mr. Bittle's competitive nature emerges, he is interested in passing on his unique knowledge to the young as a mentor. This is one of a grandfather's most important roles:

> Now, the fellers my age, I like to outdo 'em. I like to help the young folks and to give them advice if they aren't know-it-alls. But the real young kids, like my grandchildren, I tell 'em everything that I know, free of charge. I love the way they listen and pay attention. It's easy to teach them.

The gift of wisdom and experience is best applied to the young, and nature has supplied the mutual attraction—the emotional cement—so that the young are eager to absorb what grandparents have to offer. In her book *The Coming of Age* Simone de Beavoir recognized this in discussing Victor Hugo's writing about the young and the old: "Victor Hugo stated that nature supplies a spiritual communion between the child, below man's estate, and the aged person who rises above it."

GRANDFATHERS AND GRANDCHILDREN

Grandfathers have equal communion with both grandaughters and grandsons, as we will see. But they also have something special in common with each sex.

Grandaughters

Older men and little girls have always had something special between them. Charles Dickens explored the close relationship between Little Nell and her grandfather. Victor Hugo wrote about his grandaughter, "Yes, becoming a grandfather means stepping back into the dawn." He claimed that he rediscovered the world anew while explaining it to his grandaughter. Jean Valjean, in Hugo's *Les Miserables,* rediscovers his own childhood through the eyes of Cosette. Hugo's words capture the wonder that exists in the relationship between the young and the old, the mutual discovery of the magical and the ordinary. "Jeanne talks, she says things whose significance she does not understand. . . . God, the good old grandfather, listens, filled with wonder."

Nature quiets the sexual storm in men as they age. Grandfathers are easy for women to love and cuddle because women relate to them as a potent but "safe" male. The sexual tension naturally present in male-female relationships is lessened and often absent between the young and the old.

Pat, a thirty-two-year-old homemaker, told me what this meant to her. "My grandfather was wonderful all of my life. I always noticed sexual tension with men in my life, except Grandpa. With my dad, I had to be modest. My brothers, forget it, they were always trying to catch a peek at me. Sex was always there with all men. But not with my grandfather. I can kiss and cuddle him and sit on his lap and that's all there is. It's not that I don't view him as a man. He's more of a man than anyone I know. It's just that I feel safe with him."

Girls also learn "male" skills and attitudes from their grandfathers. One youngster calls her grandfather a "male grandmother." Grandfathers can offer their grandaughters a role model for maleness different from that of the other males the child meets in her daily life. Through grandfathers, young girls come to know the tender side of men.

Grandsons

Grandfathers often view their grandsons as an extension of themselves and relish the fact that they can have fun with the child. For the first time, the hard edge of the competitive and adversarial warrior system is dulled. Thus their time together is relaxed, with grandfather usually teaching, showing something, or frolicking with his grandson. Often they are conspiring against the powers that be. One grandfather and grandson I know regularly meet each other once a week during hunting season. Grandfather picks his grandson up at school after lunch and tells the teacher that it is time to "visit Granny in the nursing home." In American Indian societies, I have visited grandfathers who teach the young their ways and have fun doing it. They compete in a lighthearted way, with fishing, snowball fights, etc.

Grandfathers express profound feelings of love for their grandsons. "I love my son, but this is different. My love for my grandson is a brand new-experience," a grandfather told me. "It's a pure love. I don't have to boss him around or to train him, but I am intensely interested in his life and future, that he turns out all right. It's love that I have never experienced before. I see myself in him from outside of things, not as close as I was with my son. I think this is better. I know what really counts now, so little things that he does don't hassle me, and I don't take it so personally. I would be so much better as a father now, so I am careful. Instead of taking over, I am helping my son be the kind of father that I wanted to be.

"He, my grandson, is an extension of me into the future . . . my immortality. . . . From a selfish point of view that's why I cherish him, too."

Before discussing the special roles of grandfathers, a word of caution is in order. It is important to avoid sex-typing these roles. The roles grandmothers and grandfathers each play for their grandchildren are similar in some ways and different in others. Each of them can perform any of the roles. Grandchildren may nudge their grandparents to play a preferred role (*i.e.* making grandmother primarily a nurturer, grandfather a crony, or vice versa). Thus, when I speak of grandfather as a hero, it doesn't mean that grandmother is not a heroic figure in her own right. Grandmothers and grandfathers should not be compared with one another. In the eyes of grandchildren, their qualities are complementary and not competitive.

SPECIAL ROLES OF GRANDFATHERS

Head of the Family

As the eldest males in the family, grandfathers serve a spiritual and mystical function. As viewed by their grandchildren, "real" grandfathers are the titular head of the family, just as "real" grandmothers are viewed as the "heart" of the family.

William is a ten-year-old child who lives in Brooklyn, New York, and who spends a great deal of time with his grandfather. "My grandfather is the head of our family and everyone listens to him. He started the family meat business when he came over from Germany a long time ago. He knows a lot that we don't, and most of what he says is right. It's because he is so old that I listen to him. He knows so much more than everyone else. Who better to lead the family and make decisions for me? I trust him."

William is not the only one who feels that way. The concept of the grandfather as head of the family is present in many cultures. In the Kuru language, in Africa, grandfather literally means "my own." Grandfathers in many societies have a symbolic role. They embody a relationship that a noted anthropologist describes as "binding . . . [that] creates inescapable claims and obligations between kinfolk by reason that they are kin . . . in an axiom of altruism and amity."[4]

---

4. Martin Fortes, "Ritual Festivals," *American Anthropologist* (1936), p. 38.

As a living ancestor, the grandfather is an archivist and represents a universal figure that appears in mythology, religion, and primitive cultures as the "Old Man." Grandfathers symbolize the family's physical and emotional attachments to the dead. After all, as one youngster said, "Grandfathers are one step behind their dead relatives."

In the Tupian Indian culture of South America, grandfathers are heroic figures associated with thunder, and the hereafter is called the "Land of the Grandfathers." In the Chinese culture, grandfathers are the guardians of a long-standing tradition that views long-dead ancestors as personages with rights and duties. The actions of present-day family members are judged by the dead ancestors. It is the function of the elder to assure that homage is paid to dead ancestors. In this system, grandfather, father, and son are links in a chain of venerated ancestry that extends over time. In American Indian societies, grandfathers often name the newborn children. In the Tetum culture of South America, ancestral spirits are represented in ceremonial rites by a grandfather, and grandfathers may talk to spirits freely, seeking their advice and giving ear to their displeasures. Ancestral ghosts provide spiritual sanction for important events. Marriage and procreation occur under the aegis of ancestral spirits and are mediated by grandfathers. The "Land of the Grandfathers" is also a place of spiritual power in the American Indian religion.

In early European and Eastern history, clans were formed in order to keep property in families. Occupants of lands and castles passed on their titles and possessions to the next generation. The elder male was the holder of titles and passed them down to his progeny, both male and female. Property, whether natural (land and livestock), material, or incorporeal (names, magic, skills, charms, etc.), was transferred from one generation to another. In addition to protecting the possessions of the family, the grandfather was responsible for the identity and reputation of the family and for the behavior of its members. He fulfilled a governmental function, ensuring justice within the family. In those times, grandfathers wove the family together with common threads of family pride, reputation, property, and mutual concern and caring.

These functions are still relevant today. Though the castle has become the family business, there are many grandfathers like William's, who live according to the same principles.

Heroes

Grandfathers are heroic figures to most children. They are especially viewed in that way when they spend a great deal of time with their grandchildren in a close and intimate crony relationship. In the eyes of a grandchild, a grandfather is half real, half fantasy, a real live romantic figure of which myths are constructed and legends created. The writer Henry Fairlie, in an article entitled "Too Rich For Heroes" that appeared in *Harper's,* emphasized the importance of this dimension of the human experience: "Among all these fantasies none is more important than the fantasizing of the child's own environment, its past and its present, which it must not only people, but people with heroes . . .to see a grandfather as a hero, to gaze up from his knee and love and worship, above all to listen and to listen."[5]

Children have told me about grandfathers who played with Babe Ruth and who fought in the trenches in World War I. Because men went to war and war, at least the glamour and mystery of war, sounds romantic, exciting, and dangerous to children, they love to hear stories about their grandfathers' adventures. Because of the way that society was structured in the past five decades, men were afforded more mobility, freedom, and opportunity. On the whole, their lives were more exciting than those of homebound women, a situation far less common today. Thus, grandfathers' tales (Tolstoy used this phrase for a book title) and adventures are music to children's ears. In A. J. Cronin's work of fiction *The Green Years,* his young hero describes the beginning of his crony relationship with his newly met living ancestor: "Thus began, for Grandpa and myself, an era of glorious adventure as we beat our wings into the unknown."

Matt, nine years old, had a similar grandfather:

---

5. Henry Fairlie, "Too Rich for Heroes," *Harper's* (November 1978), pp. 36–8.

> My grandfather went out to Colorado when he was only ten years old. He worked in a tiny gold mine for some years, and he showed me some of the nuggets that he dug up there. I have one myself. To eat, he used to catch rattlesnakes and get them behind the neck and snap off their heads. Then he went to work in a Pennsylvania coal mine and he turned blue. His hands are still blue.

Grandparents are not only viewed by kids for their stories of the distant past, their current deeds are also heroic. For children, a grandfather's job, his role in the community or religious life, his friends, and his activities can also be heroic. Indeed, the child himself can be an "almost hero," as one grandfather told me, idolized in the eyes of a loving and involved grandfather who waxes eloquently over his grandchild's learning and various activities, from identifying birds to catching the "big one that got away." The grandparent is heroic because he "knows" things that others only "know about." He tells his grandkids his secrets—and that's very heroic.

Mentors

Grandfather can be a master teacher of a curriculum not taught in schools. His classroom is portable; it is the workplace, the workshop, the kitchen, or the great outdoors. Grandfathers impart information, ethics, and values that children learn nowhere else.

Milly, fifteen years old, has a grandfather that teaches her how to be self-sufficient. "My grandpa does everything by himself and he knows everything. He can cook, fix the plumbing, do carpentry, and even tries to do his own doctoring. Grandma doesn't like that. I do his income tax with him."

Max, a ten-year-old, says, "I know something is right when it feels right. My grandfather taught me how to carve and he told me that I'll know when it's right if I close my eyes and feel it. When it feels right, it is right. I can carve a block of wood so it looks like a racing car, but it has to feel like it to *be* it."

Children have told me that their grandfathers taught them

"character" and "discipline." One woman reported that she became a lawyer because her grandfather was "like Abe Lincoln to me. He taught me a sense of right and wrong—and besides, I was the apple of his eye. I always wanted to be like him."

Grandfathers and Young Children

Often grandfathers are a bit bewildered by infants. One grandfather explains:

> Well, they are cute and everything when they lie there and I like to hold my grandchildren, but not for too long. Well, first its mother is watching me closely and my wife wants the baby, but besides that, I get a little bored after a while. At the beginning it's kootchy-koo and that's about it. Now, when they grow up, that's when I start having fun with the kids. I get to take them places that I always wanted to go to when I was a kid but never could. We have a ball together. I like to talk and to hear them talk back. I guess I like the kids more and more when they grow up, but I don't like them when they're young.

Most grandfathers that I met started to really enjoy their grandchildren when the youngsters began to walk and talk. They like to do things with children. But that's only the majority. Mr. Pelner, a fifty-five-year-old grandfather, doesn't feel like that: "Heck, I can do anything my wife can for the baby. I can change his diapers and feed him. I take him for walks when I can. Infants aren't a problem for me at all, though I know most of my friends wouldn't touch them with a ten-foot pole."

THE NEW GENERATION

The grandfathers I spoke with who are uncomfortable with very young children are so because they were removed from young children during their working years. Fortunately, the new generations of grandfathers will not be ill at ease with their young grandchildren because men today are becoming more knowledgeable about child care.

The roles of grandfathers are legion and everchanging. Grandfathers of the new generation, younger and more vital than ever before, have an unprecedented opportunity to spend precious time with their grandchildren and to assume their rightful place as a guiding and protective force for their families. This is a point worth repeating, one I can never emphasize enough. It is imperative that men consider this opportunity seriously and shape their lives in such a manner that they can apply all of their creativity, resources, and the sum of the knowledge and wisdom they have accumulated throughout the years to become true grandfathers.

SEVEN

Grandmothers—Every Grandmother Has Her Own Song

Grandmothers within a close family attain enormous emotional and spiritual influence over its members. This cannot be underestimated, and it has been recognized throughout history by societies that value human relationships. In the words of an old Spanish saying, "The grandfather reigns, the grandmother governs."

Although grandmothers' praises are not loudly sung in industrialized societies, they are still a recognized force in other, more "primitive" parts of the world. Many cultures celebrate a rite of passage of women into grandmotherhood. In the Bororo tribe of Africa grandmothers are called *Umufasoni*—"Noble"—and reach the high point of their life when they are accorded that title. They are treated with highly formalized respect and politeness, and no jokes about them or quarrels with them are permitted. They are also the uncontested superior of their daughters-in-law. Grandmothers of every race and country have a legendary role as healers. Jewish grandmothers make chicken soup; others have their own special remedies. When a child in a North American Yurok Indian tribe is ill, Grandmother goes out into the wilderness to intervene with the spirits by singing and speaking to them. Every grandmother has her own song.

In Haiti, grandmothers' mystical powers are well known. They have special prestige as women born to good luck, and can make the potatoes grow, ease the pain of childbirth, share knowledge of the secrets of nature, and provide permanency among the trials and tribulations of life. People of the Ndembu religion in Africa believe that grandmother ghosts are in charge of conception. Grandmothers are authoritarian figures whose status is earned by having reared their own children, by being there at all times. A woman's life plan unfolds until she becomes a grandmother and gains the privilege of being revered, respected, and supported by all of her progeny. Grandmothers in primitive cultures expect to help raise a second family, and the family expects them to help around the house but also to provide for grandmother's needs. Children view grandmothers as wise and all-knowing, part of the way things are, "nature's helper," as one youngster said.

Like all powerful figures, grandmothers have many forms. Loving and warm to their grandchildren, they are also awesome and tyrannical mothers-in-law. There is a well-known story about a woman who was asked why she never visited her married son who had moved away to another state. She replied, "I am waiting until they have a child because I would rather go as a grandmother than a mother-in-law."

The awesome fear inspired by grandmothers has been explored by social scientists, surprisingly without tongue in cheek. Anthropologists have noted that when some young parents live with a matriarchal grandmother (which is common in many societies), depending on economic conditions, intergenerational wars abound as the battle for family territory is fought. Fear of grandmothers' "earth mother" influence and power is evident in comments found in the scientific literature: "Grandparents may bring complications into the lives of the adults around them"[6]; "Students of the grandparent generation suggest that problems with grandmothers are critical when three generations share the same home "[7]; "Don't let grand-

6. Edith Neisser, "How to Be a Good Mother and Grandmother," Public Affairs Pamphlet no. 174, Sixth Edition, 1956, p. 15.

7. United States Department of Health, Education and Welfare, "The Older Person in the Home," pp. 142–43.

parents' spoiling go unchecked; they are competing for your child's affection"[8]; "[the widowed grandmother] may be deliberately destructive of family relationships. She learns to regard her only or oldest son as a substitute for the absent husband and uses the grandchildren as pawns in the conflict between herself and her son's wife, whom she cannot forgive for taking her son away."[9] These comments indicate the power accorded a grandmother. After all, is she not the all-powerful mother grown older and wiser? Is not the classic embodiment of unbridled malice, the "evil witch," but a grandmother figure—an archetype—gone awry? No wonder she scares immature adults.

Although grandmothers' power is not often apparent in industrialized societies, it is there, deep within the hearts and minds of children and in the memories of adults. They operate as the "wardens of culture,"[10] as a "family watchdog,"[11] and as the sentinel of the "family national guard."[12] Grandmothers are the "kin-keeper,"[13] the family telephone operator (keeping people in touch with one another), and the "stabilizer of mothers."[14] Their role is emotional: feeling, supporting, teaching, and communicating—a force that is there, and that is a basic part of life. And it is this powerful force that is so attractive to children and has earned grandmothers their permanent place in the mind and hearts of the family.

A grandmother's life is a continuum, from mother to grand-

---

8. Edith M. Stern and M. Ross, *You and Your Aging Parents.* New York: W.W. Norton, 1952, p. 129.
9. Olga Knopf, "The Facts and Fallacies of Growing Old," *Successful Aging.* New York: Viking Press, 1975, p. 135.
10. David L. Gutman, *ibid.*
11. Lillian E. Troll, "The Contingencies of Grandparenting," *Grandparenthood,* Bengston & Robertson, eds. Beverly Hills: Sage Press, 1985, p. 149.
12. Grunehilde O. Hagestad, "Continuity and Connectedness," *Grandparenthood,* Bengston & Robertson, eds. Beverly Hills: Sage Press, 1985, p. 46.
13. Talcott Parsons and Robert F. Bales, *Family: Socialization and Interaction Process.* New York: Free Press, 1955, pp. 120–21.
14. L.A. Minturn and W.W. Lambert, *Mothers of Six Cultures: Antecedents of Child Rearing.* John Wiley and Sons, 1964, p. 156.

mother, until the young take over and then nurture the grandmother. In fact, many children I have interviewed expressed strong feelings that they would never allow their grandmother to be put into a nursing home.

Grandmother's fate is often rooted in her family more solidly than grandfather's. Compared to grandmother he is an outsider to the family. She has invested her life in those relationships, while his investment has been in work. Her world and power within the family expands as she grows older. His influence can diminish unless he works at it.

Grandmothers do become more assertive and more influential in the family sphere as they grow older. In fact, often they become the force against which grandfathers and grandchildren conspire.

Mrs. Mesta, a grandmother who came to America from Sicily when she was twelve years old, said that she waged "guerilla warfare" against her husband until she became a grandmother:

> I was promised to him and married when I was sixteen. I always wanted to work, but he wouldn't let me. I waited on him hand and foot, played the role of obedient wife. He worked hard for the family. I did like my mother and grandmother did for their husbands.
>
> But everyone knew who really ran things in the family. It was the older women. The men were like front men. They made believe that they were the boss, but we laughed at them. The kids were scared of the men. It was the kids and us against them . . . the grown men, when I was young. That's where the guerilla warfare came in.
>
> One day I told him that I was going to work and that's it. He said okay. Since I did that, I can talk to him on equal terms and he respects me more. I can be out in the open with what I want and we get along better. He is not threatened now like he used to be. I could have stayed the same way . . . run things from behind the scene, but when the grandchildren came I didn't want to do that anymore. I noticed that my husband didn't have any closeness with the kids, and even though he tried, he was too uptight to be with the

> grandchildren, even though they like to be with him. I broke up the old system, and it freed him, too. He knew that I was the powerful one in the family now, and I didn't want to have the old ways.
>
> One day he told my grandson that they would go out to drive together and not to tell me. He also showed my granddaughter where he had hidden some money but for her not to tell me. That was the old system. I did the same, hid things from him with the kids when I was younger and he was the bad guy. Now I have the authority and I don't want to live that way anymore. I want things out in the open and fair, fifty-fifty.

Her husband agreed: "When I was young my grandfather ould take me aside and have me sneak messages to his friends . . and I wasn't to let my grandmother know. It's funny. When my randfather was young, he was the boss. When he got older, she was. would've happened to us if my wife didn't change it."

Margaret Mead wrote: "One of my grandmothers, who always ved with us, was the most decisive influence on my life. She sat at e center of our household. Her room was the place we immediately ent when we came home from school. We did our lessons on the herry-wood table with which she had started housekeeping. Later was my dining room table for twenty-five years."[15]

Children trust their grandmothers' intuitive knowledge of the asic human processes of birth, death, and illness. "A grandmother the only person," a youngster told me, "that can stick her finger own someone's throat, look up their behind, or give them a bath . . and it's okay. No one thinks a thing about it. That's what a randmother does." In *The Psychology of Women* psychiatrist Hene Deutsch idealizes grandmothers' special qualities:

> She has renounced everything, she does not continue anything, she does not seek repetitions, she seeks no identifica-

5. Margaret Mead, "Growing Old in America," *Psychology Today* (March 1980), . 268.

tions, she is free of competitive feelings. In all her relations she is freer than at any other stage of her life; perhaps she confronts life with the same directness as a little child. She is freed from her own passions, perhaps the conqueror of them. All she wants from the world is peace; she does not reach out for the inaccessible, she wants only what she can have. She does not suffer from the split between will and ability, her gaze is not directed to any distant goal. She is now as kind as a human being who has accepted the imminence of death and as wise as only a human being can be. And because she is free of all human ambivalence, the children usually love her unambivalently, with a minimum of their own typical aggressions. [Dr. Deutsch does not ignore grandmother's power.]

She represents only one danger for the mother's pedagogic efforts: she pampers the children, but this pampering when done by the grandmother is an act of wisdom, because she is moved by kindness.

You little grandmother with a golden mind
You little grandmother with a soft heart.

These words from a Mordvin lamentation for the dead grandmother prove that the grandmother's tenderness toward the grandchild and that of the grandchild toward the grandmother, must be regarded not as a product of civilization but as a general trait of the human soul.

GRANDMOTHERS AND GRANDCHILDREN

As a rule, grandmothers do not relate differently in any major wa to their granddaughters than they do to their grandsons. Throug their grandmothers, young boys come to know and love and respec a woman without conflict and guilt . . . and they know that the lighten up their grandmothers' life without having to do anything but exist. From grandmothers, they learn the joy of unconditional love.

Grandmothers are beyond gender for young boys. Many adolescents that I spoke with said that they are much less embarrassed about things with their grandmothers. "She can see me naked anytime," John, an eleven-year-old, told me. "I don't care when she comes into the bathroom to see if I took a good bath. Grandma doesn't count that way."

For grandaughters, grandmothers can be more authoritative because they supply a strong role model. For young girls, their grandmothers are survivors, living examples that no matter what happens in life, one can endure. Sometimes a fortunate grandaughter is selected as grandmother's favorite grandchild and a "secret" pact is formed, known only to grandmother and grandaughter. Although this is an unfortunate situation for others in the family—both "unselected" grandchildren and rightfully envious and angry "unselected" parents—the privileged youngster is happy.

Millie, nine years old, is her "Gammy's" favorite grandchild. "I get the best toys at Christmas from her and she wants to take me places and not my brother and sister. It's not fair . . . but I sure have fun with her." Her "Grammy" feels guilty, too. "I know it's wrong to pick out Millie. . . . What can I say. I am just crazy about her. It's some sort of chemistry. I love the others, but I am gaga over Millie."

THE NURTURING ROLE

Grandmothers play many roles: ancestor, historian, mentor, hero, wizard, crony. But the most important and all-pervasive role is that of nurturer.

An available grandmother supplies the emotional foundation for the three-generational family. She is deeply, emotionally bound with her own children, especially her daughter. No matter what happens between mother and daughter, as parent and child, a rebirth occurs with the new child.

A sixty-year-old grandmother explained the force of this event and how it changed her relationship with her own daughter: "Frankly, Anna was not my favorite child. She gave us a hard time all of her life. That's hard to say, but it is true. When her baby was born, I stayed with her for one month to help out. It was one of the most meaningful times in my life. She told me that when the baby came, the first thing she thought about was me . . . what I went through with her in her life, and she asked my forgiveness. It was a special moment. She told me that she believed that I never loved her very much. But that when the baby came I loved her again and I loved the baby. We were so close . . . and we still are."

The relationship between grandmothers and daughters-in-law deserves mention, too. Not only is it highly complex, but a healthy relationship is imperative so that the man is not emotionally drawn and quartered between his mother and his wife. Nature has set up the possibilities for an adversarial relationship between grandmothers and daughters-in-law. The relationship needs lots of attention to flourish, and is easily bruised. The grandmother may love her "son's children" and ignore the disliked daughter-in-law. When this happens, the grandmother may lose her son. The children feel loyalty problems, torn between the grandmother and mother who are at odds and both of whom they love. In some cultures, emotions run so high in these situations that it can be fatal. Young mothers have been known to commit suicide when they are forced by their tradition to live with a tyrannical mother-in-law.

Women, because they are especially sensitive to people and relationships, have the power to create emotional havoc or bliss in their families. They are most often the keepers of the feelings of their families. This is a responsibility not to be taken lightly. Grandmothers, older and wiser, need all of their wisdom and experience to keep emotional harmony. They can do this in their role of emotional leader.

THE HEART OF THE FAMILY—THE EMOTIONAL LEADER

Nature supplies grandmothers with the ability to intuit the emotional aspects of things and to easily express themselves through their relationships with others. For children an involved grandmother can be the emotional bedrock—one living spirit—of the principles that bind the family: security, stability, permanence, wisdom, experience.

Children describe their grandmothers with eloquence: "Grandma is food." "My grandmother is the Madonna." "Granny is God if she were a girl." The sensuality and the earthiness of grandmother is well known to children: "She smells so good and is the best back-rubber in the world"; "She gives the best baths"; "I am like a flower and she is the sun"; "She cooks so good." Grandmothers' concern and caring are viewed by children as "worry." "She always worries about me when I am late from school, I know I'd better get home quick." A seventeen-year-old told me that he's angry at his grandmother because she doesn't go to sleep until he comes home at night. He wouldn't come in as promptly for his own parents, and he doesn't mind if they worry because they "are strong." Children regard grandmothers with great tenderness and concern for their fragility. "My grandmother is so sweet and dear," an eight-year-old girl said. "I wouldn't hurt her for the world."

Grandmothers earn the good grades that their grandchildren give them.

Age supplies them the natural talents for the job: life experience and confidence in what they do because they have seen the fruits of their labors—they are valued by their children and grandchildren and make them happy. Caring is the cornerstone of the nurturing function of grandmothers, and is the quality that most children feel strongly about. "I know that she cares," Alice told me, "wherever I am, whatever I am doing. She is with me. I feel her." Caring is expressed in many ways: remembering important events, upholding traditions, herding the family together, but most importantly by being together, alone with their grandchildren.

When grandmothers are not conducting the family orchestra, it can play out of tune. Or, as in the case of Phyllis's family, it can fall apart. Thus, a fifty-one-year-old, now a grandmother, recalled what happened to her family when her own mother died:

> While she was alive we all met every weekend and had a wonderful time. Her home was the family "home plate" as we used to say (because the food was so good). Whenever there was a problem between family members, she would step in and get everyone together again. I remember that one of my sister-in-laws, who is a real bitch, used to bad-mouth her. Well, my mother would be so nice to her that eventually she brought her around and they became very close. When she died, my sister-in-law took it as hard as we did, but she went back to her old ways.
>
> I tried to do the same as my mom, and to invite my family over. It's not the same, and now we sort of all go our own ways. It's terribly sad. When my mom died, so did the family.

Others have told me that their families broke apart when a grandmother was no longer available to cement family members into a cohesive unit. Several people reported that they had to wait until a beloved grandmother died to get a divorce because they dared not cause her suffering in her lifetime. The majority of people with close grandmothers hold firm the values that they have learned. These endure even after the death of grandmother. Pia, thirty-five, is "living a good life. Knowing that Grandmother is up there watching me and caring for me gives me the strength to go on when I am out of steam."

Grandmothers are powerful, and the new generations of grandmothers must realize the emotional power that nature has endowed them with. The fact is that, whether they like it or not, as twelve-year-old Dora put it, "Grandmothers are necessary."

THE NEW GENERATION

The new generation of parents and grandmothers has a great challenge before them. How will parents be able to assist their own parents, their children's grandmothers, to fulfill at least part of their natural functions? How will grandmothers use the new time and vitality that they have been given? Will they continue to do nothing, or work, or retire to a far away place, either physically or emotionally, and become a non-grandmother? Will they achieve a healthy balance between full- or part-time grandparenting and work or study? Will grandmothers respect the powerful roles that nature has given them within the family and carry out these roles? Will they have the passion and creativity necessary to overcome the barriers that exist between them and their loved ones? Can grandmothers who become involved and active find creative ways to assure the continuity of their families after they are gone? The answers to these questions are crucial and will decide the quality of the emotional future not only for parents and grandparent but for their grandchildren, who have nothing at all to say about it.

What songs will future grandmothers sing? Or will their voices be silenced?

EIGHT

Great-Grandparents—Family Icons

Over forty percent of older people live long enough to become great-grandparents. In the near future, there will be more and more great-grandparents, living longer and healthier lives. The roles and functions of great-grandparents can be compared to those of grandparents. Great-grandparents do less physically with their great-grandchildren because of their understandably diminished vitality, and the fact that they may have an abundance of great-grandchildren. On the other hand, great-grandparents are more of a storehouse of experience and wisdom than grandparents, by virtue of the fact that they have lived longer. Emotionally and physically, vital great-grandparents act very much like grandparents, except for the fact that there are two middle generations between them and their grandchildren. Since the oldest and youngest generations have a propensity to conspire with one another, this can lead to tricky situations.

Such a situation is described in *The Green Years*, A. J. Cronin's lovely story about young Robert and his great-grandfather. In the beginning, when Robert rejoins his family, his grandmother introduces him to his active and vibrant "Great-grandpa Gow." "It isn't every boy that has a great-grandpa," says his grandmother. "I can tell you. It's quite an honor. You can just call him 'Grandpa,' though, for short." In this phrase, Robert's grandmother has defined the difference between grandparents and great-grandparents, reducing the vital and frisky great-grandfather Gow one generation because of his vitality. In Gow's eyes he was too young to be a great-grandfather. Lack of physical vitality is second only to lack of emotional vitality in limiting the functions of great-grandparents. In fact, vitality is not an issue in the roles that great-grandparents play as living ancestors.

LIVING ANCESTORS

In the eyes of children, great-grandparents are important figures, living ancestors, and they don't have to do very much to gain the adoration and respect of their young offspring. Mr. Calwell is a ninety-year-old great-grandfather who serves as the "family icon." This term was coined by his great-grandson Henry, a college student who studies fine arts. Henry told me that "it's Gramps' presence alone that gives meaning to all of us. Through him we see each other. The man has thirty-five grandchildren and fifteen great-grandchildren. Do you know what it's like when we get together?"

Mr. Calwell's family is spread all across the southeastern United States and their annual family reunions fill two motels. "Great-Grandpa is the star attraction," said Myra, a grandaughter. "He is what we all have in common." Mr. Calwell lives with a grandaughter beside the sawmill that he founded and at which he worked for most of his life. His grandchildren now run the business. Mr. Calwell spends time at the mill, seated in his wheelchair. He tells "stories about the old wars and the old days" to whomever will listen. He told me that he has so many "young" that he ran out of names for them so he named some of them "Chuckloin, Brocade, Avalon, Channel, Newrail and Oleomargarine." He called his twenty-first grandchild "Twenty-one." "My wife wouldn't hear of that and gave them Christian names."

"He is a treasure to us," a grandson said. "My kids take to him like he was a new puppy dog. We take him wherever we can. He loves it. We pop him into the car and show him off." The family ignores Mr. Calwell's frequent memory lapses and loss of bladder and bowel control. "That's what happens when you're old. It'll happen to us, too, one day. Part of life." His family "will keep him with us. He wants to die in his own bed, and when the time comes, that's where it'll happen."

Great-grandparents are all living ancestors. Like Mr. Calwell, other great-grandparents attend or "are wheeled out and put on display" at family functions. They symbolize the family continuity and history, and embody the spirit of the family personality. Frequently, great-grandparents whose mobility is limited require an "emissary" to help them spend time with their great-grandchildren. Stephie is a seven-year-old who "visits my Nanny first with my Grandma and then when Nanny gets tired I go to Grandma's house. Nanny is Grandma's mother, can you believe that? Boy, is she old. . . . But she says that she was like me when she was a little girl. I'm proud of that because I love her. She has things in my family that go back hundreds of years. I hope that I can live as long as her."

OTHER ROLES

Great-grandparents can adopt any of the grandparents' roles if they have the time and energy to do so. A seventy-year-old great-grandmother, Mrs. Hanes, has "plenty of get-up-and-go." "I look after my grands and great-grands just like I did with my own." Her children, grand and great-grand, view her in essentially the same manner. "Mama is great. She's different from Mom [mother] and Grandma. She doesn't ever bother us at all. When we want her she's there, and otherwise she leaves us to Mom and Grandma. She's not as much fun as Grandma, but she sure can tell us stories about her [Grandma]. That's because she is pretty old and gets tired. All of our friends think that she is cute. We show her off because she is so old and knows so much."

Great-grandparents can fulfill the roles of historian (telling stories about the family), hero (relating adventures), and mentor (teaching skills and knowledge). Vital, energetic great-grandparents can even temporarily nurture their families. Mr. Howard, eighty-two years old, a former prison guard, lives with his grandson's family and babysits his great-grandchildren while his grandchildren work. "It's a new lease on life for me. They asked me to move in. I needed them and they needed me. The kids are great, they listen to me and we have a ball until their parents come home." The children respect their great-grandfather.

Ann, twelve years old, remembered what it was like before her great-grandfather came to live with her. "I am so happy that he's here. There is a grown-up to talk to when we came home from school, and he's no bother. He is so laid back. He's got the greatest stories. We always say that it is better to turn on Pop-Pop than the television."

GREAT-GRANDPARENT—A BADGE OF HONOR

Becoming and being a great-grandparent is an accomplishment. In many cultures long life is viewed as a blessing, an indication of grace. An abundant family is a sign of status conferred by one's progeny. Even in advanced societies this can still be the case. One lady, Mrs. Mabel Waters, incurred instant celebrity by becoming a great-grandparent. I learned about her when I was interviewing Mrs. Alice Wilkins in a retirement community in South Florida. Mrs. Wilkins had told me that grandchildren were like "trophies" to many of the communities members, and that some people were competitive as to the number and the accomplishments of their grandchildren:

> Well, one day the contest was over. Here we were bragging on the grandchildren when Mabel comes sauntering down the stairs into the cafeteria with this uppity look on her face.

> Well, let me tell you that she never gave a hoot for her children and grandchildren. Knowed her all of my life. One of the most selfish people that I ever met. Well, she comes down the stairs like a queen or something and says to us, "I have the badge of honor." She has "just become a great-grandparent and wants the respect she deserves," and "if we wanted any advice about anything she would he happy to talk to anyone now that she was the top grandmother around." Can you imagine the gall of the woman.

Nonetheless, I think I detected a bit of envy in her description of Mabel's achievement.

THE NEW GENERATION

The time new generations are devoting to family is increasing. As of this writing, it appears that a new baby boom is in the making. Thus there is a good chance that more and more of the new generation will actually be great-grandparents in their lifetime. This can be a boon for the family if the new generations strive to become not only dedicated and loving grandparents, but great-grandparents as well. Children will be very pleased. As far as they are concerned, the more adults they have that love them, the better.

PART II

Birthright and Legacy: How to Make It Happen

NINE

Assessing the Family—Agenda for the New Generations

How is the new generation, now aware of the importance of establishing and maintaining as close to a "natural" family arrangement as possible, going to do it? What can people do to overcome the personal, social, and cultural obstacles to forming a new "natural" family?

These questions give rise to an agenda for the new generation. The purpose of the agenda is to establish a close family arrangement that can endure daily stresses and be a source of love and support for all of its members.

To do this, the new generation must know how to assess the state of their own family, how problems evolve, how to identify the nature of problems, and, most importantly, how to resolve them.

At the Beginning

The seeds of success or failure for the new three-generational family are sown long before the new child is born. The quality of the relationship between a young couple and the future grandparents can make or break the new family. A good in-law relationship, with open communication, a spirit of mutual understanding, sensitivity to one another's feelings, habits, and "weirdnesses" (as one son-in-law said), can create an open and welcoming environment for the new baby and an optimistic start for the three-generational family. The closer a new family tries to adhere to the ideal, "natural family" model, the better. And if the future parents and grandparents are lucky enough to be endowed with altruism and vitality, that's better yet.

A bad in-law relationship starts things off on the wrong foot and immediately sets up a conflict situation between in-laws when the baby comes. After all, everyone wants to spend time with the baby. For some it's no fun if a disliked in-law comes in the same package with a brand-new baby.

Ideally, future parents and grandparents will have settled most of their major emotional differences, clarified their roles, and come to terms with their relationship to one another. If parents and grandparents are clear about their roles and the new distribution of authority in their lives when the baby comes, many problems can be prevented.

A close and understanding family system will usually deal successfully with many of the minor conflicts that can destroy a weak family. Issues such as the grandparents' spoiling a child, family feuds, competition among children, favorite grandchildren, jealousy, and other problems inherent in the human condition—the normal human miseries—can be handled by frank and open discussion. Major problems, such as death, divorce, and serious personality clashes that cause a great deal of emotional turmoil, may test everyone's coping powers to the maximum, but strong families can survive these stresses intact. In weaker families, where members have strained relationships and are unable to talk things over with one another and work out their problems, any crisis can tear the family apart.

THE CONTRACTUAL FAMILY

There are two major factors to consider when dealing with family problems. The first is the nature of the problem: What's wrong? The second is how the family reacts to it: Is the family united or divided? This depends on the type of family. Earlier I discussed the "natural family," an ideal emotional support system for all family members. It contrasts with another type of family arrangement that does nothing much for its members, and will hopefully be used by the new generations as a negative model, one to avoid. I call this a "contractual family system." The contractual family is formed of individuals who are blood related and may present all the outward trappings and appearances of a real family, but have only the form of a real family, not the substance.

During my research I was unpleasantly surprised by the number of families that functioned in this manner. The following are some of the most common characteristics of the way in which the contractual family works.

The contractual family operates as a nuclear unit, its members isolated from one another. Parents are responsible for rearing their own children. For child care, they prefer to use "paid strangers" rather than family members. Family members primarily form attachments to friends and colleagues of the same age, and are isolated from both older and younger people. The middle generation runs the show. All too often an individual's self-worth and self-esteem are determined by the outside world (job, wealth, etc.) rather than by family standing. When difficulties arise, family members easily cut themselves off from one another emotionally and become estranged.

Children in such circumstances are often insecure. Many of these youngsters told me that they do not feel important to their parents. "I don't know why they had me," one said. Their childhood is abbreviated; they want to grow up fast. "It's no fun being a kid," such a child told me. Children view themselves as a burden to often overworked parents. They are encouraged by their parents to "grow up" quickly and are rewarded for being "independent." Such children are isolated from their elders, who spend their time doing other things, and are vulnerable to believing media-induced sterotypes of the aged unless they adopt an older person of their own choosing.

Often youngsters in contractual families are reared in caretaking institutions even though family members are available. Children of these families are also bewildered by the emotional distance between family members. They wonder why their grandparents and parents are not closer, and fear, with reason, that they will repeat the same emotional arrangements and one day become isolated from their own parents. Without a direct relationship to their own grandparents, they adopt their parents' view of their grandparents: If their folks don't like their grandparents, why should they?

Even though they may be a cause of the problem, parents feel isolated and are often at odds with their own parents, especially if their parents left them or are unavailable to them. They turn to friends to create support groups—artificial families—because their own family is not available. They express disillusionment about family life because theirs is barren, and they feel angry and guilty about it. Marriages are often under pressure to do too many things because there is no one to "spell" tired parents. These pressures can stress a marriage to the breaking point. The nuclear system, as one father said, "is a hell of a way to raise a family. Everything is on my back, I do it all. I work, come home and take care of the kids while my wife works the night shift at the local hospital. I don't like my wife's parents and I don't want to bother with them, but I tell you, we sure could use some good grandparents in this family."

Overburdened parents find it easy to institutionalize an ill grandparent rather than caring for her or him at home. "She is no use to me," one angry parent told me bluntly about her mother. "Why should I take care of her now that she needs me? She moved away to retire when I needed her to help me with the kids. Now that she's sick, she's back. Well, to hell with her."

Grandparents in contractual family arrangements essentially abandon their grandchildren. They greet the birth of their new grandchild with ambivalence. They spend token time with their own children and grandchildren and prefer to associate with people of their own age, often their own sisters and brothers. Except for ceremonial visits, they have essentially left their children. Their priorities are elsewhere. Young grandparents are sometimes "embarrassed" about being a grandparent. "I'm too young," one grandfather said. "Now that all the secretaries at work know I am a grandfather I won't be able to fool around with them anymore." "I am too young to be married to a grandfather," another commented. With increasing age, they complained about loneliness and depression. One grandmother told me, "I guess I should have taken the opportunity when I was younger to be closer to my kids and grandkids. Now I am alone. . . . I really need someone. . . . I have no one since my husband died. I don't really know my own family. There is nothing left for me to do but die."

The family described above has no cohesiveness, no center, and no personality. Elders have no cementing role. As a group, it has no past, present, or future, no master plan. In this family arrangement, altruism, kindness, interest in another's welfare are viewed as "intrusive," "controlling," "stifling," "meddling." Some people from this kind of family avoid other family members who are not of equal "status." Marco, a second-generation American, told me that he avoided his "foreign" parents and grandparents because he was trying to make it in the WASP world. "I can't bring my parents anywhere. . . . I don't like saying this, but I am ashamed of them." Marco does not value blood ties. Status, achievement, and social success are his most important possessions. He views his elders in functional terms: they are disposed of when they no longer serve a purpose. Emotional attachments aren't important. "Lots of my friends are like me: after success. I like people if they can help my career. When I meet someone, I say, 'What can he do for me.' My family . . . they can't do much for me." Because they are not rooted in their family and its history, members of contractual families are easily homogenized into the society in which they live and adopt the currently existing mores and ways. They are assimilated in one generation. Family members prize "independence" as the greatest virtue.

Some people belong to contractual families unwillingly. Lillian, thirty-four years old, was raised in a "a wonderful, warm family." She married Bob, who came "from the coldest group of fishes that I ever met." Lillian's outgoing personality and vivaciousness was frowned upon by Bob's family, who prided themselves on being unemotional, "independent." "I felt awful with them. They have no closeness, no interest in what Bob and I are doing, and his mother couldn't care less about the kids. All they care about is how they appear to the outside world. They don't give a hoot about one another. If someone is in trouble they 'let him stew in his own juice.' . . . Bob's father actually said that about his own son when he asked him for help."

The contractual family arrangement can be changed, because the family is a dynamic unit, constantly adapting to events and individuals and assimilating new information.

In fact, a new grandchild can change a contractual system just by being born and giving family members, new grandparents, and parents who await the opportunity a chance to start over.

One of the great tasks confronting the new generations is to forge an agenda for creating a family arrangement that adheres as closely as possible to a "natural" model.

The first thing for you to do is to examine the current status of your family arrangement. What model does it most resemble?

The second is to change it for the better.

Take a moment at this time and examine the status of your own family:

1. What kind of family arrangement do you have at present? What parts (people, family philosophy, attitudes, etc.) of the ideal do you have available? Is your family available geographically? If they are, how do you get along emotionally? What is your family philosophy?
2. What kind of family arrangement would you prefer to have?
3. How can you make that happen?

There are many people that live in contractual family arrangements and take it for granted. They don't know that there is something better. Often they refuse to make an effort to change things because the obstacles—geographic, economic, emotional, attitudinal, etc.—seem insurmountable.

This is not necessarily the case at all. Once you have made an assessment of your own situation and formulated a plan to make it better, it is only necessary to know how to deal with the conflicts and problems that you have identified in your assessment to begin to make things better, no matter what your situation.

To help, I will discuss common attitudes and situations that cause conflicts and problems among family members, and will show ways in which they may be resolved. Hopefully, you will be able to apply this knowledge to your own family situation.

The rewards are very much worth the effort.

TEN

How Problems Evolve

Conflict among human beings is expected and understandable. It is built into human nature. Conflict situations are, in fact, learning experiences. They afford the opportunity for different people to learn about one another's attitudes, behaviors, and philosophy of life. Conflict is an integral part of life itself, and is not necessarily bad.

For example, in-law relationships can be a breeding ground for conflicts. Personal attitudes, the forerunners of conflict, affect relationships even before a young couple marries. Do the intended spouse and the future in-laws like each other? Is Mother angry at losing her son to another woman, or is she gaining a daughter, someone new to love? Is Father angry at the man who took his daughter from him, or is he delighted that he has acquired a new son? Does the young couple intend to go off on their own to start a new family, or do they intend to include their parents in an extended family? Is there a conflict between their parents' view of their intended spouse and their own? Are they jealous of each other's family attachments? Do their families get along with one another?

Even the wedding can be a trial. People naturally have different values and different ways of doing things. At the very least this can cause an ongoing emotional tug-of-war between people who are close to one another. Disagreements among individuals and families about the time, place, invitations, and finances of a wedding can leave deep emotional wounds that fester on for years. Afterward, conflicts can arise over how often the young couple visits family members. Whom do they spend their holidays with? How do they balance their personal, work, and family time? Are their parents allowing them time enough to start their marriage off on the right foot, or are they inflicting "guilt trips" on them?

And then along come children.

Do grandparents accept and enact their new role with enthusiam and joy? Are they helpful or critical and sensitive? Do the new parents include the grandparents in their new family, or do they isolate themselves? Are grandparents helping too much, or too little? Are they spoiling the grandchildren? Are the young parents and grandparents working at ironing out their differences in personality, life-style, values, habits, and philosophy in order to get along well?

All of these are normal questions that new couples and their families must address.

FROM CONFLICTS TO PROBLEMS TO FEUDS

I have noticed in my clinical work that personal and family difficulties unfold according to a pattern. When temporary and benign conflicts remain unresolved because people can't or won't address them, they become cemented into problems. Problems then become built into the relationship, and can become more resistant and difficult to resolve than the conflicts that caused them in the first place. They take on a life of their own. When problems aren't resolved, a prolonged quarrel—a feud—occurs.

This is a three-stage process. The first stage, open warfare, is conflictual. When this is not resolved by open confrontation and communication, a second stage occurs. Incapable of dealing with their differences, separating the problem from the person, the participants withdraw from one another. I call this "shunning." In the third stage, estrangement, the relationship becomes moribund.

It is important for you to become familiar with the workings of this model and to use it as a guide to identifying, assessing, and resolving your own conflicts before they evolve into more serious problems.

OPEN WARFARE

In this stage of the conflict, one or more of the parties involved announces dislike of the other. Contact between the people involved is emotional, angry, and often noisy. Feuds can occur between anyone in the family. For example, Marcy Wells, twenty-five, and her brother George, thirty, are examples of people who, according to their mother, "never got along." "I can't stand his guts," Marcy shouted to me when I spoke with her. "He is loud, obnoxious, bossy, and thinks that he knows it all." George described his sister as a "narrow-minded, flea-brained, prissy, motor-mouthed, card-carrying jerk." "When they are together, the sparks fly," their father lamented. "It's like when they were kids," their mother said. "I'm supposed to judge who is right and who is wrong. Sometimes they are both right. My husband just tells them both off."

In open warfare, family members are usually asked to choose sides. The family becomes polarized. "Of course they both have their way of looking at things, and I can understand where they are coming from. But they don't talk to each other. They go through us. I have a hard time with it," Mr. Wells said. "I worry that someday they will stop talking to each other for good."

Mr. Wells's worry is well founded. If people locked in open warfare don't do something to rectify things, they proceed to the next stage of their feud—shunning.

SHUNNING

When a person is shunned by an individual or a group, he or she is ignored and relegated to a state of nonexistence. Thoughts and feelings are not directly expressed, but smolder within. Shunning is difficult for all family members, because relatives are often forced to choose sides and the problem is compounded.

Mary Liz, twenty-nine, was feuding with her mother-in-law, Frieda, fifty-nine. Their long-standing feud started early in Mary Liz's marriage, when Frieda felt that Mary Liz was too "possessive" of her son, Ken, and "led him around by his nose." Instead of discussing their feelings directly with each other, they complained to others, who eventually repeated back to them the "terrible things" they had said. Without direct communication, they avoided each other "like the plague," as Ken put it. They both were invited to attend Frieda's niece's wedding. Mary Liz didn't want to go, because Frieda was going to be there. Ken was angry at her for being so adamant about not going, and angry at his mother for causing the rift in the first place. Frieda had "never liked Mary Liz from the moment I met her." Mary Liz told me, "I was sick to my stomach a week before the wedding. I had to go for my husband's sake, but I swore I wouldn't talk to his mother. My two kids were invited also, and I knew they would want to see their grandmother and talk to her. My husband takes them over there once a week, but I have nothing to do with them. I never want to speak to her again. She never accepted me from the beginning when I wanted her to love me, and now she can go to hell."

Some people shun one another for a lifetime. Lee Maypole lived one block away from her father for thirty-five years. He passed her on the street often but would never speak to her. "I married against his will. He said that I was too young [seventeen] and he didn't like John [her husband] and me marrying out of the religion. Now here we are still married. But my father never gave up his grudge. My kids would go over to see him. When we attended family affairs, he looked right past me. He wouldn't even do that until my mother threatened to leave him." Mrs. Maypole started to weep when she told me that her father wouldn't talk to her even when he was on his deathbed. "He was dying at home, and my mother needed help to care for him. He told her that I wasn't allowed to help. My brothers and sisters were there at the end. . . . I watched them care for him. I tell you, I hate him for that; I will never, never forgive him." Her mother told me that Mr. Maypole was "proud of

Ann and would worry about her when she wasn't well. He loved the grandchildren, too. He was just too hard-headed, too much a thick Irishman, to forgive and forget. He hurt the girl deeply."

When shunning occurs, the parties are not totally estranged. They communicate with one another by means of an intermediary, a message carrier, like Lee Maypole's mother. The intermediary, often annoyed and frustrated with both people, becomes the keeper of the relationship. That's what Mrs. Maypople did.

"They drove me crazy talking about each other all the time. It was like an obsession. I tell you, I was as hurt as both of them. It caused a row between my husband and me, and I would have left him except that he was such a good person otherwise. He told her before she got married that she didn't have his blessing and that he wouldn't talk to her again if she didn't have the respect to honor his wishes. He prided himself on being a man of his word, but it caused all of us a lot of pain. May he rest in peace."

Shunning may be the preferred way that certain families deal with problems. Mrs. Maypole told me that two of her husband's brothers hadn't talked to each other for many years and that even when the children fight "they don't talk to each other for weeks at a time."

Sometimes the message carrier gets fed up and forces the parties to confront one another. Father Ruiz, pastor of a church in the Southwest, got fed up with the complexities of coordinating confirmation arrangements for Teresa Montoya. Teresa's father, Joe, was not talking to her grandfather, Mr. Torres. Father Ruiz couldn't find a mutually convenient time to have the ceremony because of all the squabbling between Joe and his father-in-law. "I got mad," Father Ruiz told me, "and told them to come in here and talk it over with me. They refused, so I went out in my car, found Joe, brought him to Torres's house, and told them to straighten out. They were ruining Teresa's confirmation. Well, they started talking after that."

Individuals who shun one another without being fortunate enough to have a go-between or the will to re-unite on their own eventually become estranged from one another.

ESTRANGEMENT

Estrangement signals the death of the relationship. In some cultures and ethnic groups, banished family members are considered dead and are formally mourned. The emotional fireworks of open warfare and the covert guerrilla warfare of shunning fizzles out. Even the negative feelings become dulled with the passing of time. The parties eventually become emotionally distant and socially isolated, consciously relegating each other to the remote past, where memories are dimmed.

John Foster became estranged from his son Jerry "thirty years ago. Jerry was eighteen when he left. He was acting like a bum so I told him to shape up or ship out. One day he just upped and left. His mother became distraught, and she never forgave me for being so harsh. Jerry's sister is in touch with him sometimes. I told her not to talk to me about him. I feel terrible about him. . . . He was such a cute kid. I try to keep it all away from my mind." Jerry's sister was sad about the situation and angry at her father and brother. "They could have considered my mother and me more. I lost a brother and lost respect for my dad. I think they both killed my mom. They were selfish. Their battle hurt a lot of innocent people, even my kids. They have an uncle somewhere who they never met."

In the next chapter, we will examine some common conflicts and problems. New parents and grandparents, especially, should be alert to the difficulties I will describe and quick to remedy them, before shunning and estrangement develop.

ELEVEN

Identifying the Problems of Quantity Between Parent and Grandparents: How Much Grandparenting?

The new generations will encounter many conflicts that will put them at odds with one another, both personal—attitudes, values, sensitivity, life-styles, etc.—which result from the basic differences between people, and situational—mobility, divorce, stepparenting, etc.—which result from rapid personal and social change. Situational problems are usually no one's fault, yet often are the hardest for families to deal with. They do not lend themselves to simple solutions. Often, the trick is to make the best of a bad situation.

Personal problems can be more easily dealt with because conflicts between family members are normal and expected. It's the cost of doing family business, part of the way things are. In fact, with so many differences among people—temperament, personality, attitudes, sex, habits, life experience, personal life-style—and their reactions to various situations that affect them—illness, death, divorce, etc.—it's a wonder that people get along with one another at all. Although conflicts are emotionally disturbing, they also offer people an opportunity for personal and family growth. When conflicts are openly discussed and resolved, family members become closer and learn to know one another better.

Read the following pages with an eye to placing yourself in the situations of the people described. Put yourself in everyone's shoes.

Whom do you naturally side with? How would you handle the same situations they are involved in? Do any of these situations apply to you? Could they happen to you in the future? Are they happening now?

Keep in mind the following points:

1. The conflicts and problems described can be either resolved or exacerbated by the people directly involved. In most cases, family members have a choice.
2. Rarely is one person the cause of a conflict. The conflictual system is a resonating one; it goes back and forth between two parties at least, and everyone involved bears at least some responsibility, at some time, for the outcome of the conflict.
3. Conflicts are complicated. They can be ongoing—due to a difference in personality or values—or temporary—due to circumstances such as illness or socioeconomic pressures. Conflicts are more easily reversed before they evolve into problems.
4. Conflicts evolve through several stages: the event that starts the conflict; open warfare (the reaction to the event); shunning (avoidance as a method of dealing with the conflict); and estrangement. The emotional reactions to these events are surprise, protest, disappointment, despair (open warfare), and detachment (shunning and estrangement). They can be worked out at any of these points in the evolution of the dispute, but the earlier it is done, the better.
5. Conflicts among emotionally healthy people are usually limited to a specific relationship. Grandparents who may have a problem with one child or grandchild might not have a problem with other family members. Parents may have an excellent relationship with one set of in-laws and not with the other.
6. Parents' relationship with grandparents is naturally conflicted, unlike that of grandchildren. Like it or not, parents are the linchpin of the vital connection between their parents and their children. They do not act in isolation.
7. When conflicts occur, children suffer. Either way, when par-

ents and grandparents reject each other, the children lose their grandparents.

8. Outside help is available and useful. Friends, clergy, counselors, or therapists can be of inestimable value in breaking an emotional stalemate among family members. They may help a person identify and resolve a conflict with advice, or even intervene for them. A family physician can be a useful resource in finding the right therapist.

First, a warning is in order. Problems between the generations can be grouped into two main categories, but these categories are not meant for use as *absolute* cubbyholes to label or simplify complex relationships. Neither are they to be used as pejoratives or psychological curse words; name-calling a grandparent a "long-distance grandparent" doesn't help. Rather, these categories are intended as helpful guidelines. Conflicts between family members can be terribly complicated and intertwined, truly an emotional can of worms; that's one of the reasons that people run away from them. Any attempt to simplify them is inherently problematic, so remember that each category is far from being cut and dried. At least one or two other elements are contained in each category; grandparents who do "too much" grandparenting can also be insensitive. Parents who deprive their children of their grandparents may also be insensitive and have different life-styles. These groupings are diagnostic tools for learning exactly what is not working within a relationship, or a family. Only then can we start making it better.

The first category describes problems that arise among individuals. It includes conflicts about the quantity of grandparenting (too much or too little); conflicts arising from differences between parents and grandparents in attitudes, values, or life-styles; personality conflicts (mutual insensitivity); and miscellaneous problems of spoiling, favoritism, and competing grandparents.

The second category deals with the effects of situations and events on intergenerational relationships: death; divorce (of parents and grandparents); mental and physical illness; stepgrandparenting; and so on.

TOO MUCH GRANDPARENTING

This is a problem frequently expressed by parents who are overwhelmed by overconcerned and overinvolved grandparents. On the other hand, some grandparents complain that too much is being asked of them, and resent the degree of involvement that their children require.

Too much grandparenting is an exaggeration of the normal interest and joy that grandparents take in their grandchildren. Although this pleases most grandchildren, parents can feel emotionally overwhelmed. One young mother described her conflict: "I get invaded every day by my parents, and they are upset if I am not at home when they come. They even bring their friends to show them the baby. They don't think about me—my feelings and my privacy. All they care about is the baby; they are nutty about him."

Leo says, "My parents want to possess my little girl. They eat, sleep, and think Susie twenty-four hours a day. They get sick if they don't see her at least three times a week. I feel guilty when I don't let them see her. The pressure is terrible, and my wife and I fight about it. We have no life of our own. We are thinking of moving away to get rid of this problem." Like other parents I met, Leo and his wife, Janet, talked about his parents to each other incessantly and considered shunning them. "I am afraid of telling them off, too," Janet said. "I would just like to move and then we wouldn't have a problem." Hardly a good solution, and all because Leo is unable to confront his parents directly. If he did, at least he would have a chance to work things out.

Shunning and avoidance are many parents' primary way of dealing with problems with their own parents. In a mobile society, moving away is a readily available out. Charles, a thirty-seven-year-old father of three, was unable to cope with his overzealous parents. He was planning to move his family away when I first spoke with him. "I live in the same apartment building as my folks and an aunt. If my wife doesn't make the rounds and visit them every day with the kids, there is a major-league guilt trip from my parents . . .

especially my dad. 'I didn't see the kids today,' he tells me or my wife. 'Are the kids okay?' They have to see the kids when they leave in the morning and come home from work. They [the kids] are asked to perform for their company. They worry about fire, and they can't sleep when the kids are sick. It's too much. It bothers me more than my wife. She says that she likes the attention and the fact that we can take off whenever we want. It makes me whacky." Confronting his parents "would hurt their feelings. I respect my parents and I don't want to make them feel bad. How can I tell them not to bother the kids so much? It would kill them. Come to think of it, what would moving away do? It would only hurt more."

Charles is right. Grandparents have no defense against the shunning or geographic relocation of their children. This leaves Charles in a dilemma: not to confront his parents is to continue to resent them; confronting them is to risk "hurting their feelings." What Charles should do is to confront his parents with his feelings and resolve the problems. Hurt feelings are easily repaired. Estrangement leaves deep and enduring wounds.

Charles's parents, like other overzealous grandparents who can't seem to get enough of a good thing, should be aware of their own behavior. Their voracious love is swamping their grandchild's bewildered parents, who stand between them and their grandchildren. His parents would do better to observe their son's reactions to their behavior, as the following grandmother did.

"I go crazy when I see that baby," said Marge, a fifty-seven-year-old grandmother, "absolutely gaga. I can't get enough of her, but it seems that her parents are upset when I want to be with the baby. I don't know, they seem selfish, like they want her all to themselves. Lately, they say that they are going out when I want to come over. I feel that they are avoiding me. Something is wrong, and I think it's time to talk it over."

Fortunately, Marge did just that, before it was too late. Her daughter-in-law, who felt "invaded," was ready to move. Like other parents, she was not willing or able to confront the problem head on in order to work it out. By taking the initiative, Marge kept her family together. She expressed her feelings to her shy daughter-in-law, who then felt comfortable enough to share her own feelings with Marge. They decided to organize their time better, allowing Marge ample time with the baby while the parents went off alone. They agreed to get together regularly for family dinners at each other's homes. Most of all, they agreed to talk about their situation and to discuss any conflicts that arose and to try to work it out to the best of their ability.

Too much grandparenting, like too much food, can cause emotional indigestion.

Some elders feel that their children expect too much from them. This is especially true of those grandparents who are working, at school, or at rest. They may resent their children's intrusion into their own lives. "I love my kids and the grandkids," lamented George, a sixty-eight-year-old grandfather, "but I just don't have the time to work and to spend all the time with them that my son and daughter-in-law want. I see the kids plenty and I have a great time with them, but I can't make it over there every other day and all weekend." Gene and Judy, his son and daughter-in-law, "love him very much." Gene says, "He is a great guy and the kids are crazy about him. When he's here, it's a complete family. My mom died two years ago and we are all he has."

Being asked to grandparent too much is of course a relative issue. For George, who describes himself as "more or less a loner," several visits a week to his son's house would be enough. His grandchildren are not complaining, because George gives them a great deal of attention several times a week and makes a point of attending their big events. They know him through spending ample time together. The pressure is coming from his own child, Gene, who feels that his father isn't involved enough. "Better they want me than not," George says. "I guess it's not enough for the kids or grandkids, but sometimes it's too much for me." If this is all George can do, then, for the time being, his son may have to settle for it without aggravating the situation further. At least the children aren't suffering.

TOO LITTLE GRANDPARENTING

The unavailability of grandparents to grandchildren is a common and serious problem. There are many reasons for this, and grandparents and parents may both be at fault when this occurs. Grandparents may not fulfill their roles, either because they don't want to (they are disinterested) or because they can't (work, distance, illness, etc.). Parents may not want grandparents near their children because they dislike them (feuds) or because of the insurmountable inconvenience; they may be unable to arrange their lives to get the generations together (work, distance). Some well-meaning grandparents aren't as available as they would like to be simply because they have too many grandchildren and there is just not enough of them to go around.

Grandparents Who Don't Want to Grandparent

Grandparents who don't care enough to grandparent cause a great deal of distress in young parents and grandchildren. Some shortsighted grandparents allow their negative feelings about an in-law to come between their grandchildren and themselves. Myra, a mother, aged twenty-three, complained about her mother-in-law. "She never says how gorgeous our baby is. We pack up the baby and take her for a visit to Grandma's, and Grandma just talks to my husband and ignores me and the baby. She drives right by our house when she goes to work and never comes in. I don't understand this. My mother is crazy about our baby, but she lives a thousand miles away." Mrs. Wooley, Myra's mother-in-law, knows why she doesn't see her grandchild more often: "I don't like Myra. Never did. I didn't want my son Tom to marry her in the first place. I want to see the baby alone but Myra comes along with it, so I don't see the baby more. Besides that, I have a lot of friends at work and I enjoy them and like to spend time with them. It's more fun." Mrs. Wooley is acting in an immature and narcissistic way. The only way Myra can hope to change the situation is by calling in a third party that Mrs.

Wooley respects, perhaps a clergyman, and having him mediate between them.

Hal, thirty-two, has a mother who "doesn't want to be a grandmother." "She has a fit when we ask her to babysit. She says that she raised us and now it's our turn to 'sacrifice.' I guess that she wasn't a happy mother. It's like she resents me. She sees taking care of kids as a drudge and a worry. When she comes she is constantly talking about the baby choking on food, falling down the stairs, or drowning in the bathtub. We all miss having a grandmother." His mother said she feels like she has "other priorities. I feel free for the first time in my life and I don't want any responsibility now. I've got other things on my mind."

Uninvolved grandmothers are not the only ones who draw their children's fire. "My father would rather hang out with his cronies," Jane, thirty-eight and mother of four, said angrily. "He doesn't work anymore and would rather play with his friends than spend time with my kids . . . and they adore him." Her father said he feels that he's earned some "peace and quiet."

Many of today's grandmothers have been "liberated," and offered a new lease on life when their children grew up. Some have abandoned their families in their newfound liberation. One father would have preferred that his mother be a traditional "Granny . . . yes that's what I hoped she'd be. That's one of the reasons I haven't moved, so she could be with the kids. Y'know what she does now? Well, she's divorced from my father. She dates, leads an active life . . . she works part time and she is going for a graduate degree in philosophy. She's like a roadrunner. She comes here once in a while to pay her dues and then she takes off again." His mother feels that "This is the first time in my life that I can do what I want, and I'll be damned if I don't take advantage of it. I guess I'll have to sacrifice seeing the grandchildren. I really love them, but they are not in my priorities now." One of her grandchildren, Steven, eight, is resigned to the fact that "my grandmother is great. She is a lot of fun but she is a busy person and doesn't have time for me. If she liked me enough, I guess she would." Steven expresses what many grandchildren feel when their grandparents are vibrant and interesting and available people who are unavailable to them: rejected.

Having an available but disinterested grandparent hurts parents and children all the more, especially when a grandparent is sorely needed. Grandparents are very important for adopted children, especially at the time of adolescence, when many adopted children test their parents' love and commitment to them. "My parents have never taken to the kids that we adopted," June, a mother with two adopted youngsters, told me. "I felt a sense of failure that I couldn't have my own. My parents didn't help. They said that the kids aren't of our blood. I understand that, but the kids don't. They love their grandparents, and the kids are terrific. But my parents don't want to be bothered. We all feel pretty bad about it. I don't think I'll ever forgive them. It's hard to say, but I hate them for the way that they are acting".

Wilma, twenty-seven, has a handicapped child. "Mary was born blind and deaf. My parents don't even want to see her. I can understand how they feel, but I need them and Mary needs them. They brag about their other grandchildren and don't even talk about Mary. They never help by going to the hospital."

It's not easy to get a disinterested, uninvolved grandparent interested in their families in an unselfish way. There is hope, however, and it lies in the awesome power that children possess of being attractive and lovable. The trick is to have an uninvolved grandparent spend as much time as possible alone with the children. Sometimes nature goes to work and allows the kids' love to break through the self-centeredness of the narcissistic adult. Some parents make an effort to take vacations with and visit their uninvolved elders often. Some send their children to stay with their grandparents and are "pushy" about it, not put off by their elders hesitation or excuses. As one parent told me about her own disinterested parents, "I'll get whatever I can for my kids out of my parents, whether they like it or not." One thing is sure, parents and grandchildren should keep trying. Some grandparents are slow starters and need prodding to get the relationship going. Even a little grandparenting is better than none, and the children most always benefit.

There are various other reasons why elders with grandchildren don't grandparent. Some just can't; they are too far away from their families and have to settle for being "tele-grandparents." Others just don't want to be grandparents. It is not a part of their life plan. Their biological instinct to grandparent is overwhelmed by their own selfishness or by a combination of their selfishness, their liberation from the responsibility of caring for their own children, their unexpected vitality, and the newfound opportunities that society offers to today's middle-aged people. Some are plain hedonistic; others are too busy with other things.

Stephanie, a sixty-year-old working grandmother, is representative of this new group of grandparents. She told me she "raised her kids and that's it. Look, no guilt trips for me. Let my kids raise their kids like I did. I am free for the first time in my life. My kids are going to have to cope with their families just like I did." Her son describes Stephanie as a "good and devoted mother, although she resented every minute of it." Stephanie lives in a small New England town less than one hour from her three children and four grandchildren. She views her involvement with her family as minimal. "I want to live my own life. I'll get together with everyone for holidays. I love the grandchildren. They have their own lives. I don't want to interfere, butt in, or boss the kids around. They have got their lives and I have mine. We are independent from one another. The grandchildren . . . well, I really haven't thought about that one."

Her thinking is reminiscent of the attitudes and views of many grandparents who have created contractual families and are no longer involved with their families. Whether they are involved in work, playing shuffleboard in some far-off retirement village, or isolating themselves behind closed doors, they have renounced not only their children but their grandchildren. They appear to be happy and satisfied with their lives, although their children and grandchildren miss them and are slowly becoming estranged from them.

We strongly urge these grandparents to reflect about their behavior. What are they doing to their children and grandchildren? Ask the young how they feel about the lives that their elders are leading. Parents, whether they are asked or not, must speak out and let their elders know what they are doing to their families.

Members of the newly emerging generation of grandparents can use their liberation from rigid schedules to good purpose. With our agenda, liberated grandparents can use their vitality and energy to find ways to combat the prevailing forces that separate families and assure that their great-great grandchildren will have a family to belong to in the future.

Morris and Michelle Getmin, recently liberated grandparents, moved to a small town in Vermont and used all of their savings to purchase a general store, gas station, and restaurant so that their married son and daughters and their spouses and children could live near them, together as a family. "My family was all over the place —California, Wisconsin, Arizona," Mr. Getmin told me. "I felt that the situation was ridiculous. My family was my life, and here we were all separated. I had retired from my job, had time at last to spend with my family, and I rarely saw any of my three children or my grandchildren. That's not what life's about. I decided to do something. When I talked to my kids about how I felt, I learned that they felt the same way. We all decided to have an adventure—to take a chance as a family and move to Vermont and establish ourselves in some local business. My kids are all college graduates with good jobs, but they agreed to give it a try. So here we are. It's rough sometimes, and we have to work at it, but it's going well." He smiled. "Look, I don't know how it will turn out. Some of the family may stay and some may go. But every moment that I have with all of them is golden for me. Now, at least I know my grandchildren and they know me. If I hadn't thought of this, what the hell kind of life would I have? Where would we all be?"

Mr. Getmin's solution to the isolation he experienced is a shining example of the creativity and ingenuity that the new generations will have to employ to overcome the roadblocks to family unity.

Liberated grandparents can be mobile, and, with a little ingenuity, go to their families if their families can't go to them. Monica, ten, told me that she has a "secret deal" with her grandparents. "They move when we move," she said. "We have moved three times in the last seven years and my grandma and grandpa moved right after us." Her grandmother said she "never thought that I would become a traveler in my old age, but I want to be where my family is." Monica's parents didn't mind at all. "It gets a bit hectic at times," said her father, "but we have a lot of adventures together with all this moving around. If my folks didn't follow us, we would never see them. With my job, I have no choice. If I didn't move I would be out on my ear."

Other grandparents establish a home base for regular family get-togethers. Mr. Walters, sixty, bought a summer place so his family could come to him. "I scrimped and saved since I was thirty so that I would have enough money to buy a small cottage on a lake where my family could come to spend summers with us. I had such wonderful memories of summers at my grandparents' that I wanted to do the same for my family. It's the only time in the year that I get to see some of them." The Sterns, who live in the city, use a hotel for family get-togethers. They save their money and take their grandchildren to the mountains for two weeks every summer. "That's the highlight of the year for me," said Mr. Stern. Grandparents who can't afford to move may buy summer cottages or go to hotels with their grandchildren, or do other things. Some go on schoolday trips with the children, others invite kids to their homes, whether it's a house or apartment, for weeks at a time. Liberated grandparents, because they often have a more flexible schedule of obligations, are free to do things when and how they like. And that's good for all of the family.

PARENTS WHO REJECT GRANDPARENTS

A great many of today's parents resent grandparents' intrusion into their lives, an attitude so prevalent that it has resulted in many of today's grandparents being legislated out of existence. Until recently, courts shortsightedly viewed the family in terms of only two generations—the "nuclear family unit."

Grandparents lose their rights to their grandchildren most often in disputes with their own children or when an in-law gains custody of a grandchild through divorce or death.

Petey Donaldson was nine months old when his father, Rolf, was killed in an auto accident. After Rolf's death, Dalia, his wife, finished college and got a job. The Donaldsons looked after the youngster and supported Dalia, whom they loved. Three years after Rolf's death, Dalia married a man she had met at work. The Donaldsons were happy about it and glad that Petey would have a father. "I was glad that Dalia found someone to love her and Petey," Mrs. Donaldson told me. One year after the marriage, Dalia's husband legally adopted Petey, and the Donaldsons have not seen him since. "Our hearts were twice shattered," said Mr. Donaldson tearfully. "Once when we lost our son and again when we lost our grandson." "I don't want any of the old memories," said Dalia, "and the Donaldsons are part of the past. I don't want to be cruel. They were good to me. I just want to start over. My new husband doesn't know them. Petey will forget them. He's got my parents and my husband's parents now."

The Donaldsons, however, have not forgotten their grandson. They went to see him at school and were told by the principal that they couldn't do that. As the Donaldsons became more adamant, Dalia got a court order barring them from seeing Petey. There was nothing the Donaldsons could do for eight years, until their state passed a law giving grandparents the right to sue for visitation. They went to court, and lost their case. The court said that it had been too long a time since they had been close to their grandson and that the child didn't know them well. It was also "inconvenient" for the parents to have to manage Petey's time with the Donaldsons. The Donaldsons were ordered to cease and desist in their efforts to reunite with their grandchild. "We live near one another and go to the same church," said Mrs. Donaldson, "but Petey is not allowed to come near me and vice versa. I see him in church sometimes, sitting with his other grandmother. He peeks at me when no one is looking. He remembers."

But it's not only in-laws who cause problems. Cheryl feels that her parents were "self-centered and bossy with me when I was growing up. I fought with them all of the time. I don't want my kids exposed to them and their ways. I don't want my kids to suffer with them like I did." So Cheryl keeps the contact between her parents and children down to "a minimum. They can send birthday presents and see them on holidays, but that's it. I don't talk to them at all.

My parents call and ask what can they do, but it's too late now. I feel that I am doing my kids a favor." Her husband doesn't totally agree: "They don't seem that bad to me. Their other kids seem to like them. But I can't take their side—Cheryl gets too wild. She's got a deep wound because she feels that they screwed her up."

Cheryl's parents are very disturbed about her attitudes. "We never got along too well. She was a rebellious kid, into drugs and drinking when she was young. We fought a lot, but you'd think that was water under the bridge now. For her the battle still is going on." Her father reflected a moment. "We are being cheated out of our adorable grandchildren."

Cheryl's children told me that they didn't understand why they couldn't spend time with their grandparents. John, twelve, told me that his mother "freaked out" whenever he mentioned them. "I don't know, it's best that I just keep quiet, but I like them and they seem real nice. Maybe I'll know them better when I get older and my mother can't bother me about it." Maybe not. Although many children involved in these feuds have secret thoughts about re-uniting with their grandparents when they are older, and some have certainly done it, the fact remains that grandchildren and grandparents alike are being cheated out of the most important years in their relationship. Feuding adults should be aware of how their behavior affects their children and how they lose face in the eyes of the youngsters when they cannot settle their own problems. At very least, it "isn't fair," as so many kids have told me, "to treat a kid like this."

Visitation between a grandparent and grandchild should never be permanently stopped, for the simple reason that people can change. If they want to, grandparents and parents should try to be forgiving for past transgressions, forge out a set of guidelines for future behavior, and afford one another the opportunity to learn from their past mistakes, instead of being eternally punished for them. Try again. Do it with supervision, if necessary. Parents must make a maximum effort, no matter how justified their animosity toward grandparents, to respect the integrity of the grandparent-grandchild bond. It is cruel not to do so, and it is the child who ultimately pays the price.

With an increasing divorce rate, a high rate of mobility, and a decrease in the importance of family bonds, more and more grandparents are being unwillingly separated from their grandchildren. Overworked parents feel they have no time or energy to be bothered with getting their parents and children together. "I am too tired to worry about that," Cindy said. "I work from nine to five, run a house, and try to do the best I can with the kids. If my parents want to see the kids, let them do something about it, but I don't want them butting into my affairs or telling me what I am doing wrong. I have my own life to live and I want to live it by myself." Grandparents who care are hurt and angry when this happens. Open warfare occurs. "She's a very selfish person, Cindy is," her mother shouted. "She only thinks of herself. I can't drive, so I can't get over there. There is no public transportation where I live. She's not interested enough to get me over there. I have these lovely children who love me and that I am nuts about and we can't get together." "Sure I'd love to see Grandma more," said Arlene, a ten-year-old, "but I can't. No one has time to drive me over to her apartment in the senior citizens' place. I really miss her, too. I love being with her. We all [the two other children] do."

Like other youngsters deprived of their grandparents by their parents, Arlene cannot express her feelings. "How can I tell my parents how much I love my grandmother? They get mad at me when I say anything, so I keep quiet." Her mother said, "I don't want to hear how much she likes her grandmother. I haven't got time to do it all. Sure I tell her to stifle it. . . . I guess it makes me feel guilty, but I can just do so much." But Cindy could do better. She could arrange for a friend to take Arlene to see her grandmother. Fortunately, grandchildren are part of the solution to many problems. They become more independent as they grow older. Arlene will soon be able to take a bus to her grandmother's house alone.

At one extreme, and totally neglecting the effect of their attitudes on their children, some people are actually happy that grandparents are "out of their hair." Jill, a thirty-six-year-old mother of four, was delighted that her parents weren't available to her children. "Thank the Lord," she said with a smile, "they moved to Florida, a thousand miles away, and I don't have to deal with them. My parents have moved away to retire. Ha! Ha!" Her youngest child,

Bill, doesn't think it's very funny. "I love my Grandpa especially. We did so many things together, had so much fun. I don't know how he could leave me. I miss him. He was my secret pal . . . that's what we called each other. I never see him anymore." For Bill, a grandparent who drives his mother crazy is not his problem at all. Perhaps if Jill knew how he felt, she would value her parents more. Bill is a bit too young to tell her all by himself. Fortunately, her oldest child, Allen, sat his mother down one day and told her how unhappy he was with her attitude toward his grandparents. "That got to me," Jill said. "I still can't help my feelings, but I will keep them to myself now. I just never thought about my kids. I was too busy being a kid myself."

PARENTS WHO STAY CHILDREN, GRANDPARENTS WHO STAY PARENTS

When a new baby comes along, both older generations have new roles to play. "I changed the way that I acted toward my son Don the day he became a father" said Paul Evers. "I knew that I had to respect and support him in his new role, like my father did for me. After all, he's watching out for my granddaughter, so I'll watch out for him." Paul noticed the difference. "My Dad has changed since Amanda was born. He's less bossy, and he praises me more. He's more respectful, I guess."

If grandparents don't fall into their new roles as grandparents but continue to remain parents, treating the new youngster just as if it was their own child, conflicts arise. This relegates the new parent to perpetual childhood. An angry young mother told me that her son called his grandmother "Mamoo" one day instead of "Gamoo" and that her mother-in-law, "Gamaw," liked it so much that she didn't correct the child. "I am the mother, not her. My husband doesn't think that it matters, but it does to me. I am jealous, and I am the mother." Gamaw should respect this. After all, Gamaw is Gamaw.

Sometimes kindness and dedicated interest by a grandparent can cause an insecure parent to back off and relinquish the parental role. Ella, a twenty-one-year-old mother, felt that her mother could "do it better. She's got more experience at handling babies. She is a kind person. At the beginning, it was great having her help, but slowly she took over and I did less and less. Whenever she's around, I back off. I don't want to, but I don't want to argue with her. She whisks Billy away from me when it's time for his bath, and feeds him and changes the food I give him. I feel like I'm not doing it right."

Often grandparents have to assume parental roles when parents are unavailable. The trick is for a grandparent in this situation to be able to switch back to an advisory role when the parent returns to full duty. If not, grandparents risk shunning as parents move away in an attempt to resume normal relationships with their own children.

Sally and Joe moved in with their parents when Sally decided to go to nursing school. Joe worked as a night watchman. Their parents, the Probarts, were happy to help them out and especially to have the two boys, Art, eight, and Jake, five, at the house. After several months, Joe noted that the boys asked their grandfather for permission to do things, even when Joe was present. They also asked Grandfather to play games with them. "I always had fun with my kids. I feel jealous that the old man is replacing me. He even asks me if I want to join them, like I was the older brother. Not only that, but he interferes when I discipline the boys, and it's none of his business." Mr. Probart feels that "it's my house and we do things my way here. I think that Joe is harsh with the boys, and I don't want that when they are under my roof." Sally was also distressed: when she asked Art to clean up the dishes after lunch one day, he told her that he didn't have to do it because Grandma said that "he didn't have to do anything that he didn't want to."

After one year, the hostility increased to the point that Sally left nursing school and went back to work so that they could move out of her parents' home. "It was unbearable," she said. "Not only was I fighting with my parents, who wouldn't listen, I was fighting with my husband, who was complaining to me about them. It was a mess. The kids were suffering, too. They didn't know who to listen to, who their parents were." The Probarts were "shocked that they left. I still don't know why," Mrs. Probart said. "I thought that we just had some minor disagreements." Mr. Probart had some idea: "I think that Joe was jealous of the way the boys took to me. If I had it to do over again, I would handle things a bit differently . . . let him be the father more. I think I overstepped my boundaries a bit. I blew it." "I'm afraid this situation has permanently affected the way I feel about them," Sally said. "They screwed up, as far as I'm concerned." Art was bewildered as to what had happened. "I don't know why we moved out. I was really happy there. Grandma and Grandpa were always there, and I had a great time with them. Now I'm alone a lot, and my parents are not around when I get home from school. My dad's sleeping and my mom goes to class."

Many of the cases where grandparents have lost access to their grandchildren are rooted in the fact that grandparents who were called upon at one time by their own children to act as primary caretakers did not relinquish that role when their children were ready to be parents.

Jane left her two girls with her parents after she divorced her husband. She decided to go to the mountains of Wyoming to "find herself." She had little contact with her children for several years. One day she appeared on the front steps of her parents' home and demanded the return of her children. "I was ready when I came back," Jane said. "I had done it all and grown up. I was going with Jack and ready to take over the kids." Jane lived with her parents for a short period of time, but found it "intolerable. They treated me like a third child, not as the kids' mother. They had no respect for me. They disagreed with what I did and criticized my way of doing things." Her parents felt that they had good reason to criticize her. "She smoked pot and she was going with a bum," her father said. "I'm afraid that he will abuse the girls." Jane moved out with the children and kept contact between her children and her parents to a minimum. Eventually, when she stopped visitation completely, her parents took her to court. They lost the case. Her mother became severly depressed and spent several years under psychiatric care. "I'll never recover from what happened or understand how my own daughter, whom I love, can take those kids from us."

What is unfortunate is that Jane's parents weren't sensitive enough to take a positive view of Jane's motivation and to support her in her motherhood. This could have been a mutual rallying point. People often do for their children what they won't do for themselves. Family counseling could have been very helpful to them in settling their differences.

The damage done by failure to assume the new roles a grandchild demands is never slight. At best, parents and grandparents shun one another; at worst, grandparents are legislated out of existence. The children, bewildered and helpless, are silent witness to the antics of their elders. They do not understand why the people that they love most in the world are at odds with one another. They are frightened that a similar fate awaits them with their own parents when they grow up. They lose respect for their parents because they usually view their "old and nice" grandparents as benevolent victims, allies against the same parents who rule their lives and can deprive them, even if it's only of cookies or extra television time. The family becomes permanently shattered.

This doesn't have to happen at all. Understanding, tolerance, and compassion can help a great deal. Communication is critically important. It should be evident that many of the problems described here have a great deal in common. The people who didn't talk to one another directly and chose to complain to others, to suffer their distress in silence, or to move away, emotionally or physically, didn't solve their conflicts. Those who were direct, innovative, and involved others if they couldn't deal with the issue alone, worked the problems out. Others settled for partial solutions and were flexible enough to "trade-off," to compromise on issues in order to maintain family tranquility.

Those who work out their problems possess two basic skills that the new generations need to learn so they can help their families resolve problems: to talk directly and openly with each family member, and to be flexible in attitude and behavior.

TWELVE

Identifying the Problems Of Quality Between Parents and Grandparents: What Kind Of Grandparenting?

The topics that families fight over and the seriousness of the battles are limited only by the boundaries of human nature itself.

Some parents' complaints about grandparents center around the crony relationship that grandparents enjoy with grandchildren. They play a light-hearted game of cops and robbers with the middle generation. Parents are the cops, grandparents and grandchildren the robbers. This game can be very upsetting to insecure parents who feel responsible for their children's safety, values, and personality formation, and, being new at it, do not have the secure perspective that the long view of experience confers on grandparents.

A young mother was angry at her father-in-law because "my baby only has six teeth and Grandpa gave her a pickle to eat. He said that her expression was cute when she bit into it."

Elsa, twenty-eight, complains about her husband's father, who "takes my son into the woods and teaches him hunting. I don't want my boy around guns." Grandfather feels that "I am trying to teach Bobby to be a man. He is perfectly safe with me. His mother is a nervous person, scared of her own shadow. If I teach him the right way to use firearms, he will never get hurt with them." "That's not all that he does." Elsa has a laundry list of complaints. "He gives Bobby toy guns for presents and chewing gum that is make-believe chewing tobacco. Bobby spits it out, just like his grandfather. It's disgusting. Worst of all, Grandfather tells Bobby not to tell me what they do together. That I really don't like."

Peter, forty, a farmer, is angry at his mother, who drives his kids around town in their pickup truck and "never uses seat belts no matter how much I remind her, chew her out, or threaten not to let the kids go with her. The kids like to jump in the straw in the back of the truck and I want her to belt them in tight so they won't fall out."

Parents frequently complain that grandparents do not support their views or respect their wishes concerning the children. There is a natural urge in parents to homogenize their children's experience. They expect grandparents to treat children exactly as they, the parents, do. Although this is understandable, it is unreasonable. Children learn well from different ways of doing things. Nature has endowed children with a strong capacity to adapt and to learn from different people and situations. As long as there is no danger to life and limb, parents shouldn't concern themselves with most of the things that their children do with grandparents. But when there is danger, it must be dealt with.

Some grandparents abuse the license that their children give them with the kids. A new mother complained that her mother-in-law "does what she wants with my baby behind my back. She gives her sweets instead of meals. She even went against the doctor's advice and gave my baby cereal when the doctor said not to. She tried to toilet-train my niece when my sister said no. She's a nice person and was a fine mother, but she is unbearable—a tyrant—as a grandmother."

Other grandparents inappropriately unite with their grandchildren against the parents. This is a pathological exaggeration of the normal crony relationship.

Paula, twenty-four, said that her mother was not very happy about her having a child. " 'You can't afford a kid,' she told me, and 'you won't know how to care for it.' I was so happy and excited when I was pregnant. After the baby came, she baby-sat and taught the baby to say 'stupid Mommy' and 'stupid Daddy.' Of course my baby would laugh. She seems to love the baby all right, but she hates me.

When we are together she announces my faults to my husband and the baby, too. She makes me the brunt of her lousy jokes. I've told her how I felt many times. My husband has too, but she doesn't try to change. Now she's got my daughter doing the same thing."

Paula's mother-in-law, like all grandparents, should take their children's complaints seriously. When grandparents don't listen, they are in jeopardy of losing time with their grandchildren, and justifiably so. Why should a young and vulnerable parent like Paula submit herself to constant abuse?

Some grandparents, parents say, are just plain stubborn.

Bertha, a thirty-five-year-old recently widowed nurse, explained that her husband's parents were "bossy, critical, and inconsiderate," but she needed them to look after her three children while she worked the late shift at the hospital. "I leave at three in the afternoon and tell my in-laws to see after the kids homework and bedtime. But as soon as I leave, they all head out the door, straight to the ice cream store. And one of my girls doesn't need ice cream, she's a blimp. They could care less about making sure that the kids do their chores and homework. They visit their friends often to show the kids off. Naturally, the kids love the fuss that everyone makes over them. They have even kept the baby up so late that she was awake when I came home one night at eleven-thirty. One Christmas they kept the kids out past midnight looking at decorations. I came home and there was no one there." Her mother-in-law is concerned that Bertha is "too serious" and that she "doesn't have enough fun. The kids are happy. It was terrible when my son died and we were all depressed. Now we are trying to brighten the children's lives a bit. Have fun. Bertha is too protective. I understand, however, and she is a devoted mother. She should have more faith, however, that we would never hurt the children in any way. We are just doing our thing with them." What frustrates Bertha is not their good intentions but the fact that "they don't listen to me. They should at least hear me out and honor my requests, some of the time. There is no give with them. It's only one way, and it's their way. I can't do anything about it short of cutting them off from the kids, but I could never live with that. The kids would never understand."

Bertha, in her frustration, has neglected to look for what may be a possible solution to her dilemma: invoking a third party. In fact, the family is quite close to their local pastor, who could be of considerable help in her situation because her in-laws have respect for him.

Competition between a parent and grandparent for the loyalty and attention of a grandchild is not unusual. Everyone wants to be special to a child, and most people have a secret wish that a beloved child would love them best. With insensitive people, this natural and best ignored contest for the child's allegiance can get out of hand.

George, thirty-eight, couldn't believe what went on between his wife and his mother-in-law when his first child arrived. "When we brought the baby home my wife asked her mother if she would like to give Amanda a bottle. Her mother looked at my wife and said, so help me, 'Aren't you jealous that I'm holding the baby?' I couldn't believe my ears. My wife didn't react, and my mother-in-law repeated the same thing over again. The next week while she visited and was playing with the baby, she whispered, 'Amanda likes Grammy better than Mommy, doesn't she.' I couldn't believe she said that. I thought that she was going bonkers. Since then, and in spite of the fact that we all talked about it together, she often announces that Amanda is her golden child and that they have a 'thing' for each other . . . this right in front of my two sons. That's not all," George continued. "My father-in-law's not perfect either. He argues with me in front of the kids. He told my middle child that if he picked his nose it would get bigger. I told my son that Grandpa was wrong. So the old man takes my son aside and tells him that I don't know what I am talking about and that he knows better because he's older. What do I do about this?" After a while George figured out a solution, harsh though it was. He told his in-laws, with his wife's cooperation, that if they didn't "quit their negative and critical behavior they could only see the kids once a week." He was surprised at the result. "Boy, did that work. My father-in-law was especially shocked. He never knew things were that bad. Well, for him they weren't."

Although this is a harsh alternative, it may be worth trying in some cases. The possibility of being separated from their grandchildren can shock insensitive grandparents into using their common sense. But I would never recommend actually carrying out the threat.

Some grandparents feel that parents are insensitive to their need for time with their grandchildren. Many grandparents are relegated to obscurity when their child or ex-in-law remarries. Their grandchildren can end up with six grandparents. Parents who are insensitive to the love that exists between their children and ex-in-laws can break the hearts of the abandoned grandparents.

Parents should plan their lives so that children and elders have time together. When distance is a problem, this can be done on a daily, weekly, or even yearly basis. Remember, parents need time alone too, and grandparents are the best people to give them that time, while they get to know their grandchildren.

On the other hand, grandparents who are not in good physical health don't have the necessary energy to spend long hours with their grandchildren.

Nanny Bennett, seventy-two, a grandmother of fourteen, feels badly that she can't be the type of grandmother she would like to be, but is also unhappy because "they all want a piece of me. I can understand. But although I love them, I just don't have the energy. It's too much for me, but I don't have the heart to refuse, and then I get grouchy and cross." Her daughter Sally, forty, is aware that she is inconsiderate of her mother's health. "What else can I do? I want the kids to know her before she dies. She is a marvelous lady. If I'm not pushy, the kids will never know her." "But if you don't stop pushing, I'll be going quicker than I'm supposed to," her mother replied.

It's helpful to have someone else available when frail grandparents spend time with their grandchildren. Nancy, eleven, goes to visit her chronically ill grandmother with her parents or her aunt. "It's good for both of us. I play with Grandma and then I can talk to whoever is with me. I help Grandma do her cooking and chores, but if she's is very tired then I make dinner with whoever has taken me to see her."

Surprising as it may be to some grandparents who view their juniors as arrogant or insensitive, parents naturally expect their elders to be considerate of their feelings and patient with their shortcomings. Parents, when all is said and done, view elders as teachers, trained by experience. Parents feel that grandparents should understand them—their own children—by being loving and supportive. For parents it's more of a one-way street.

Many parents feel that grandparents are unaware of their insecurity with kids and the awesome responsibilities they bear. One of the most poignant situations I have encountered concerned a fifteen-year-old unwed mother, Ardith, whose boyfriend, the child's father, was killed in an auto accident. They had planned to marry. The young mother was very upset because the parents of her child's father did not acknowledge her son, their grandson. She had tried to get in touch with them and was rebuked over and over again. "I can't understand how they wouldn't want to see this adorable baby. They are his only living relatives except me," she said. "What kind of people are they?" Fortunately, her pediatrician intervened and got Ardith and the baby's grandparents together.

Parents must be sensitive to the fact that grandparents have special needs in regard to their grandchildren that parents might view as frivilous. One immigrant grandmother I met was upset because her son and his wife objected to the fact that she wanted to teach her grandaughter to speak Portugese and to teach her the "old ways and family recipes." She felt it important that this knowledge be passed on to her grandaughter because this was an essential part of her identity, her roots, and herself. Her son and his wife would do well to respect the grandmother's wishes. Where else could their daughter ever learn another language in such an ideal way?

ATTITUDE AND LIFE-STYLE DIFFERENCES

The recent pervasive changes in our values and attitudes, sexual behavior, women's rights, and the decline of religious influence, to name a few, have radically changed our society in a short time. Generations live in markedly different worlds. This makes for conflicts between generations that do not take the time to learn about each other's world experience. Differences in attitudes and values can grow into full-blown intergenerational wars when family members are intolerant of one another's views and assume a critical and judgmental attitude. In these matters, what is "right or wrong" or "good or bad or better" really doesn't matter. These problems are as common as the situations that spawn them.

Issues of sexual preference can easily foul an intergenerational relationship. Joy, thirty-five, lives in a homosexual relationship with Elsa, thirty-two. Elsa has two children from her marriage to Jim, whom she divorced two years before she moved in with Joy. They are both raising her two children. Joy and Elsa, regular churchgoers, are "raising the kids the best way they know how." Jim, the children's father, doesn't mind. "They are both nice ladies and the kids seem okay. They call Joy 'Aunt Joy.' I guess they ignore the other part of it. No one in their school knows what is really coming down." But Joy is upset because Jim's parents, Mr. and Mrs. Montez, the kids' only grandparents, won't let her near their home. They tell the kids that their mother is a "pervert" and "crazy for living with another woman." Joy is especially chagrined because she is "trying to make a life for myself. I'm a good person, a damn good nurse, I don't hurt a fly and yet I'm damned by the kids' grandparents." Mrs. Montez is adamant on the issue: "I don't want anything to do with Elsa. I despise her for what she has done. I'll find a way to see the kids a lot, but I never want to lay eyes on Elsa again." Nothing more has happened, despite the intervention of the parish priest, who has a more compassionate view of the situation than does Mrs. Montez.

Grandparents who aren't up-to-date can live "old-fashioned"

lives that don't pass muster with their contemporary children and in-laws.

Sandra, twenty-eight, was raised in New England and married Harry, who is from Louisiana. "My in-laws are nice enough, but they live in a shack near a swamp. They use a chamber pot and an outhouse, and bathe in a washtub. I didn't believe it either until I saw it, but I swear it's true. The only hot and cold running water in the house is in the sink. Their yard is strewn with old beer cans, automobile parts, a rusted tractor, and Lord knows what else. Food is left on the table for days. There are cigarette butts everywhere. I asked them how they live this way and they told me that they are very happy just the way they are, thank you. The problem is that they want me to leave my kids there over the summer now that they are old enough. Don't get me wrong. I like them. They are good people, sweet and kind. And smart, too." Harry, her husband, confessed to being "embarrassed about the way that they live. It sure ain't like Boston. But it only bothers outsiders." He continued, "I understand how Sandra feels, of course. My father feels that living like this is his way. He can put on the dog like anyone else. He wore a dinner jacket when I graduated from MIT. He's an original. He loves the country and sees no reason to change his ways. My kids love it here."

Sandra's distress is understandable. Like other parents, she is concerned with health and cleanliness as far as her children are concerned. Sandra dislikes the disorder of her in-laws home, but that's no reason to deprive her child of their influence. She has a great deal more in common with them than she has differences. They share the same values of family commitment, altruism, learning, and charity, things that a youngster should learn. Because of the joy her children experience with their "Louisiana grandfather" she would do well to look the other way and ignore the "mess."

But sometimes parents, like Carrie, can't just look the other way. She is angry at her mother-in-law, whom she describes as a "pig." "She cleans her house once a month. It's filthy. The furniture is soiled and she couldn't care. The floors are so filthy that I don't want my child to set foot in that house. I never use her bathrooms, and I am afraid to eat the food that she brings over. I tried everything to get her to clean up the place, but she doesn't listen. If I want it done I'll have to do it myself."

What Carrie should do is find out what is wrong. Her mother-in-law may simply be depressed. The family doctor might be needed.

Some parents complain that their elders are too fastidious. "I can't do anything at her place. It's like a hospital," a young mother complained. "I am afraid to use the toilet or her sink for fear of spoiling her showplace." "My daughter-in-law is the champion slob of the world," said Sam, a grandfather. "Her house is a pigsty. I can't find anything when I go there. Nothing is where it should be. How can she live like that? And with my grandchildren. I should call the Board of Health, except that she is a lovely person." Grandchildren have opinions, too. "My Gramma is a clean freak," exclaimed Peggy, fourteen. "When I come back from riding my horse, she makes me take a bath, even if I am not dirty. She even went out to my stable and scrubbed the horse's stall with a brush and soap and water because she said it was horrible. She's funny. She hates germs".

The important thing that parents and grandparents must remember is that they are all entitled to live in their own distinctive ways. Live and let live. The grandchildren will survive their idiosyncrasies. The question is, is it dangerous for children to be exposed to these ways? If it is, then action should be taken, and fast. If not, looking the other way is a small price to pay for such invaluable companionship.

Discipline can also be an area of confrontation between generations. We have evolved an ethic of "spare the rod and spoil the child" to the point that it is now against the law in Sweden to spank kids at all. That wasn't the way it was, even in the recent past.

Daisy, thirty-one, has problems with her discipline-oriented dad. "My dad is a swell person," she said, "but he is too harsh with my kids. He never really hits them, but he has harsh reactions when the kids foul up. He gives them a little swipe when they do something wrong. Twenty years ago he did the same to me. I must say, however, that the kids seem to mind it less than I do."

One grandmother lamented, "My God, I can't understand how Sally can take the guff her kids hand out. I tell you, I would fill their mouths with soap faster that they could blink their eyes if they ever talked to me like that." Sally was unaffected by her children's verbal torrents. "Better out of their system then holding it in. They'll sleep better." "Modern times, modern times," her mother sighed.

Religious issues can cause problems, too. Many people today have moved away from traditional religious beliefs and affiliations. Others have switched from one religion to another. Religious grandparents often feel that it is part of their solemn duty to inculcate their grandchildren in religious ways. This is a powerful spiritual function of grandparents that many feel is of vital importance. When parents are religious or follow a different religion from their parents, difficulties can arise.

Laura, thirty-five, feuds with her parents because she married an agnostic. Her parents are pillars of their local church. "They are angry at me for marrying Tom. He doesn't want the children to attend church, and my parents are upset about this. I don't care one way or the other. I just want peace. Of course, the kids would rather sleep in Sunday morning. They do like the 'fun' part, though, when they get to go with my parents. I'm upset because my parents won't talk to Tom because of his attitude toward religion."

One father told me that his very orthodox parents refused to have anything to do with their grandchild because they disapproved of her mother, the woman he'd married. "My father told me that if his grandchild isn't of the same religion then he isn't his grandchild—period." He is still hoping his parents will "come around."

It is understandable when grandparents get upset about this. "It bothers me," said one grandfather whose son married out of his faith. "Religion is community and gives me inner peace. It gives me strength. It's part of my humanity. It makes me sad to think that I can't share this with my grandchildren, take them to church with me and share the holidays. I am hurt that I can't discuss the Bible with them in an informed way. They won't know what I am talking about."

Parents should allow their children to learn about and participate in the religious practices of devout grandparents. They should not be viewed as a threat by parents but as a part of their children's spiritual education. On the other hand, grandparents should be alert not to criticize the beliefs of their grandchild's parents or comment on their differences. This will soon alienate the child. With this caution, everyone wins and parents and grandparents will get along better without this barrier between them.

Differences in habits can cause turmoil. "My parents drink and smoke like crazy," an upset mother exclaimed. "How can I leave my kids with them? They have a mangy cat and a dog with fleas that sleeps on all of the beds." A grandmother angrily shouted, "The jerks. They are raising my grandchildren with booze and pot in the house. One time I went over and found my son stinking drunk asleep on the couch and the baby crying in the crib." Callie, thirty-two, told me that "Grandpa Bill is great except that he is hell on wheels when he drinks. One day he left the baby in the playpen all day with a soiled diaper. Another time he let my three-year-old toddle down to the lake all by himself. The lake is full of alligators and Grandpa knows that. If that isn't enough, he has taken my oldest son up flying in his plane several times when he was drunk as a skunk. Even my son got scared. Not about his flying—Grandpa could fly in his sleep—but about his drinking. Grandpa did all right with the eight kids that he raised, but he scares the hell out of me." A grandmother from Arizona reported that her daughter and son-in-law "smoke like chimneys around the children. My grandkids are going to get lung cancer. You would think that their parents would have enough sense to spare them all that secondhand smoke."

Some of the habits I have discussed are part and parcel of the diversity of the human experience and the color of life. Children learn from all this. Action should be taken, however, if children are endangered. Parents shouldn't "smoke like chimneys around their children" and Grandpa Bill should be grounded when he's drinking. And certainly keep the kids away from the alligators.

Both grandparents and parents should be alert for real danger. If danger is present, intervene quickly to protect the child. Once this is done, the problem should be identified and discussed. If the problem is serious, appropriate help should be recruited. Remember, the point is to separate the good from the bad, to get rid of the problems in the relationship and not the relationship. Grandpa Bill's family got him to join Alcoholics Anonymous. Callie went to Alanon first and after a while of "working on him" she "forced him" to go to a local AA meeting. He stopped drinking three months afterward and hasn't had a drink since then.

The examples cited amply illustrate the diversity and abundance of intergenerational conflicts. There are more yet. The following section shows how the most natural inclinations of the best-intentioned people can get them into trouble when they do not listen, are intolerant of the other's point of view, and are insensitive to their needs.

SPOILING

Many parents who are reduced to a competitive relationship with their child vis-à-vis their parents freely express their feelings of envy. "My parents were strict and harsh with me," Mildred, a mother, said. "With my kids they are generous and laissez-faire. I am jealous because they haven't changed the way that they act towards me at all. My kids get whatever they want. No questions and no hassle." Her father said that he had "changed since I got older. I have a chance to spend time with my grandchildren and I really get a kick out of them. I don't have to train them and to set the rules. I can just be a grandparent—a guide. I give them more time than I give my own kids. It's easier. The grandchildren don't fight with me. They don't want more than I can give, and they are happy with whatever I can do. It's a perfect, made-in-heaven relationship. They love me for what I am." Mildred was reconciled to her father's relationship with her kids. "I am not going to stand in the way. I'll swallow my envy of the fun that they have together. I guess I feel a bit left out."

On the other hand, some grandparents abuse their license to indulge children. Lucy, twenty-five, is angry at her in-laws, who she feels are abusing their "spoiling rights." "A little spoiling is okay, but my mother overdoes it. My son cries when he leaves my mother's house. He doesn't want to come home with me. That makes me feel terrible. She gives him expensive presents and takes him places that we can't afford. They don't do that for me, mind you! Once I went shopping with my child and my mother. He wanted a balloon and I said no. Two minutes later, there he was walking around with a big red balloon. Granny got it for him. What can I say? I'm the bad guy."

Most people agree that "a little spoiling is okay." But when spoiling is intertwined with family competitiveness, a youngster can become the prize in a major competition. Parents feel undermined and become diminished in the eyes of their children, who view their own parents as the villains.

Sal, a ten-year-old, said, "My grandparents are great. They get me what I want and take me where I want to go. My parents never do that. My father is lucky that they're his parents. I get along with my grandparents better than my own parents."

Often parents who are frustrated with grandparents who spoil their kids threaten to separate them from their grandchildren. One grandmother views this as a "punishment. So I didn't use the car seat and I did give the baby what she wanted for dinner and I do keep her up late—what's the big deal. Now my daughter won't let me babysit with her anymore." Her daughter is "ticked off with the way my mother is ruining my kid. Either she changes the way she acts or she's had it—no more Danny."

Although the possibility of a grandparent spoiling a grandchild is built into the relationship, it doesn't have to happen. Parents should be aware that grandparents also love their grandchildren because they are their own children's children. Grandchildren are a living representation of the parents' love for the grandparents, a gift. Ask any would-be grandparent impatiently waiting for a grandchild about this. In the best of relationships, an adversarial system between parents and grandparents can be avoided by a wise and understanding grandparent.

Mrs. Bristol, a new grandmother, knows about this. She said, "My grandchild is a gift to me from my daughter, Penny. I know this. I also know that I could be a better mother than she can because I have had the experience, but I can't do that. It's her turn. I must be in the background and help her. Sure I could show her up when Millie [the granddaughter] is older. I had a secret deal like this with my own grandmother. She used to wink at me and make faces at my mother when her back was turned. I would get what I wanted from my grandmother when my mother wasn't around. But that wasn't good for my opinion of Mom when it was a serious thing, like money. Grandmother bought me things sometimes my parents couldn't afford, but she didn't help my parents. I saw my grandmother as the good one and Mom as strict and fussy. I won't do that with my own family, but I must tell you that the situation is a natural set-up, especially if parents and grandparents don't get along. Children can be used as ransom in the battle between them, all right. But I won't do that. I want Penny to know that one of the reasons that I love Millie so much is that she reminds me of Penny as a child, and the truth is that I love them both . . . the same love in a different way. God made it easier to love grandchildren because they don't get you up every night. It's all so much easier with grandchildren."

FAVORITISM

Nature creates some children in the image of one of their grandparents. The resemblance may be physical or temperamental, a like personality, or even a shared talent. When this happens, a grandparent feels a strong attraction to the child, often to the detriment of their children and the other grandchildren. A grandparent thus smitten has to act very carefully.

Sometimes it is very difficult. Lottie, a fifty-nine-year-old grandmother, is "crazy to a fault" about little Evelyn, her four-year-old granddaughter. The problem is that she ignores Evelyn's older sister and brother. When she comes over, she brings one present for each of the other kids and five presents for Evelyn. "I can't help it," Lottie told me. "I am nuts about Evelyn. I see myself in her. I am not happy about the situation. I feel bad for the other kids, but Evelyn is and will always be my number-one grandchild."

"My father is a male chauvinist. He always wanted a grandson," Joan said sadly. "I have three daughters, and now that my sister has a boy my kids never see their grandfather. He spends all his free time with my little nephew. I feel as rejected as the kids." Her oldest daughter, Kyle, thirteen, misses her grandfather. "He just dropped out of sight when my cousin came along. Everyone knows it. I guess men are like that. We used to have fun, but I don't see him much anymore." When grandparents pick favorites, it can divide a family and create a great deal of animosity and even rivalry between the parents of their grandchildren. Joan told me that she was angry at her sister for having the baby, "stupid as it seems." Her sister said that she feels sorry and guilty that her father is acting like this. "What can I do?" said Grandma. "That's the way Grandpa is. I'll make it up to the kids."

Children who aren't favored suffer when they aren't "picked" by a grandparent. Chris, seven years old, feels bad that "None of my grandparents picked me as their favorite. All my brothers and sisters are picked. They get to do things with a special grandparent and I don't. I don't know if I did something wrong. My grandparents do things with me but they don't seem to have their heart in it, and my brothers and sisters always say they have such a good time with my grandparents . . . and I don't."

Although favoritism seems a benign issue, it can be hurtful to grandchildren and to parents who take the grandparental rejection personally. This is understandable. As I have said, grandchildren are a precious gift that parents give to grandparents. Everyone wants their gifts to be special and cherished. A child is eager for its grandparents' attentions. When this is not freely given, or is given in greater abundance to a sibling or cousin, the unfortunate child is deeply hurt. Grandparents should be especially sensitive to doing their utmost to give all of their grandchildren equal time and love.

COMPETING GRANDPARENTS

Hopefully, grandparents with grandchildren in common will operate in a complementary fashion. Nature has given each child four—or more, where second marriages have extended the family—grandparents, four chances to have a vital connection. When this works, it makes everyone happy. When a new baby is born to their children, the new grandparents, former strangers, through no choice of their own, become indirectly related to one another. Their genes have joined together in the form of their new grandchild-in-common. Whether new grandparents recognize it or not, the quality of their relationship is an important factor in the family constellation. When they cooperate, they enhance their family and relax their children and grandchildren. When they compete with one another, everyone loses.

Mary Lou Whitely, fifty-seven, describes herself as a "selfish grandmother" who is "so crazy about my grandaughter, Paula, that I don't want anyone on the other side of the family to mess around with her head." Mary Lou doesn't care for her son's in-laws. In spite of the fact that she likes her daughter-in-law, Elsie, she feels that her son married "beneath" him, and that her child's other grandparents are "lower class." The Deans, Elsie's parents, feel the same way. Mr. Dean resents the Whitelys' "uppity ways" and wants to "get my grandaughter away from them as much as possible so I can show her what life is really about. They take her to that country club and dress her up and show her off. I like to take her fishing and to the beach and just walk around with her and let her be with real folks, not them country-club snobs with the big cars." Mr. Whitley wants his grandaughter to "have all the best. The less she is with the Deans, the better. They're not like us. It kills me when she's over there and I could be doing something with her." Paula's parents fight with each other about how much time the child should spend with each set of grandparents. In fact, they have set up a time schedule and monitor it closely so each grandparent has "equal time." Paula "loves all my grandparents. Sometimes they ask me who I love best, but I say I love all my grandparents. I do. I think it's funny the way that they try to get me to say that I love them best. I don't take them seriously. They are different, but that's fun for me. It never gets boring." Her parents are, as Elsie said, "in the middle. It's a big source of tension for Mac [her husband] and me. You can cut the air with a knife when they are together. It hurts Mac and me very much. When Paula's around, they are competing for her attention . . . it's really awful. It's not that they are bad people, but where Paula's concerned, they act like children."

It would behoove Elsie and Mac to call a family get-together to discuss the problem, with the help of a trusted friend, doctor, or clergyman, if necessary. This shouldn't be difficult, because it's a "positive" problem—too much of a good thing gone bad. Paula's grandparents would be a formidable asset to the family if they cooperated with one another.

When grandparents compete for the child's attention, the vital connection is easily short-circuited, and parents are the most likely to absorb the shock. Legend has it that the mother's mother is the primary grandparent. Although this may be a strong likelihood if the mother's mother is available, it is not true all of the time. An altruistic, dedicated grandparent will always be involved with the grandchildren.

Competitiveness between grandparents for the attentions of their grandchildren doesn't happen all at once. It usually is the result of a long-standing competitive relationship that is rooted in the personalities of the grandparents. It may start when the couple marries and their parents begin to vie for who will be closer to the couple. Whom does the couple spend their holidays and vacations with? Where does the couple live? Is everyone happy with the answers to these questions? If not, there may be danger ahead. When grandchildren come along, the field of competition is extended. Whose presents are better? Who has more money? Who can do more for the kids? The list is endless.

Dr. Lindsey, a grandparent we know, never buys his grandchildren presents before he knows what the other grandparents have purchased for the children. "I don't want to be outdone by them," he said. "If my son's in-laws take the kids to Europe for a summer, then I will take them to Tahiti the next summer. I don't like my son's in-laws, and I won't let them take the kids from me. I frankly resent the time that my grandchildren spend with them. I don't want them to influence the kids."

Dr. Lindsey's fear, like that of other competitive grandparents, arises from his worry about losing his influence over his grandchildren and of being loved "second best." Parents should take a very active and assertive role in pointing out competitive behavior among grandparents. One mother we know was so exasperated with her child's grandparents' "competition that she put a ban on all gift-giving, "even Christmas one year. They got the message."

Grandchildren who are the object of such a competition become insecure and inauthentic in their actions with their grandparents. What nature has created as unconditional love is distorted when grandchildren serve as the prize, judge, and jury in their grandparents' popularity contest. It's easy for children in this situation to become materialistic and to take advantage of the bounty offered them. Their love is no longer freely given but doled out according to how much their grandparents can do for them and buy for them. This situation becomes a travesty of a true vital connection.

Parents are sometimes forced to choose sides with their own parents against "the other side." Priscilla, thirty-four and the mother of three children, got involved in a fracas where her parents and in-laws were in a "potlach competition for the attention of the kids. They tried to outdo each other. I told them to stop, but they wouldn't listen. Whatever I did, one of them was hurt. I couldn't win. My husband and I fought because we defended our own parents. We had to go to a marriage counselor, who told us to straighten out our own parents. That helped us get together, at least. Finally, we told them to stop competing with one another or they couldn't see the kids. That helped."

Cooperative grandparents, respectful of each other's emotional attachment to their children and grandchild-in-common, form a strong and secure foundation for the three-generational family. Not only do they offer their grandchild a plethora of love and uncomplicated attachments, they also can help one another in relation to their own children. When Beth, a young mother of two, had a falling out with her own rather strict and formal parents because they disapproved of the way she "let the kids run wild," it was her mother-in-law, Sarah, who acted as catalyst and helped Beth and her parents iron out their differences. Sarah was aware that she could have been "Grandma number one" because Beth was shunning her own parents. But rather than staking a claim to the vacated emotional territory, Sarah kept that space open until they could fill it once again. "It was touch and go for a while," Sarah said. "Beth and her parents were very angry at one another and for a time I thought that they would go their own ways. I took things into my own hands, called up Beth's mother, and took her out to lunch. I told her to take the first step and to call up her daughter. In sum, I gave her a boot in the rump. She did it and all's okay now. Sure, I could have ignored the whole thing. Beth was actually confiding in me and getting closer. I could've shut out her parents if I wanted to. Beth was vulnerable. But I'm not like that. They are part of Beth's family . . . so that makes them part of mine."

Parents with four involved and supporting grandparents have a powerful support system. Parents with competing grandparents have, as Priscilla put it, "four more babies." Fortunately, the positive forces contained in competing grandparents can be harnessed by sensitive parents for the good of the family. What is necessary is openness and forcefulness and the ability to draw the line. Stopping the competition by banning presents, for example, might be a good, temporary way to make the point.

What helps most in overcoming these difficulties is when people, recognizing their differences but affirming their commitment to one another, listen attentively to the other's point of view, tolerate and respect the right of the person to that point of view, and negotiate differences quickly, before conflicts become more serious, deeply rooted problems.

When conflicts occur, family members should be especially careful to avoid being caught in the crossfire of the intergenerational war—children between their parents and grandparents in visitation issues, parents between their children and their parents when either generation is angry at them, and grandparents between their children and grandchildren, especially common when teenagers feud with their parents.

It is important that all feuding adults pay strict attention to how children are affected by witnessing or being directly involved in the conflicts of their elders. What is the child's role? Is the child a prize in the competition between adults. Is the child ransom, used by one adult to manipulate the other? Is the child being accorded undue authority by an adult who needs the child's approval for one reason or another? All of these situations are harmful for children and damage their respect for their elders.

THIRTEEN

Identifying Special Problems That Arise Between Parents and Grandparents

There are countless other situations and circumstances that affect parent, grandparent, and grandchild relations. In this chapter I will discuss some of the most common issues. Among them are mental and physical illness of a parent or grandparent, divorce, and step-grandparenting, taxing situations against which the new generations will have to shelter their families.

MENTAL AND PHYSICAL ILLNESS

Illness profoundly affects the normal structure and rhythm of family life. Lines of authority are broken, and role reversals may take place. Even a temporary illness can have long-term effects on family relationships. A family's members may cease to function, or may function in such an aberrant manner that the whole group is thrown into turmoil. As one youngster said, "What good is a grandpa with Alzheimer's disease?"

Sometimes family members mistake a temporary illness for a permanent change in the person afflicted and change their attitudes toward him. Fortunately, when the problem is identified, most parents and grandparents can rebuild a relationship marred by an illness.

Minna, a fifty-seven-year-old grandmother, described herself as being "grouchy and miserable for two years. I was no use to anyone. I was angry and critical with my children, in-laws, and grandchildren. I thought it was my age and that I was getting old and grouchy. Soon after I started behaving like this, people started drifting away. Then one day, I collapsed. The doctor diagnosed a thyroid disease, and after a few weeks of treatment I was myself again. I almost lost my family in the meanwhile." Her daughter agreed. "My mother really changed her behavior. No one knew that she was sick. I thought it was her . . . and that she was just growing old. Her grandchildren didn't want to be near her anymore because she was so grouchy. They were quite upset about her. If she didn't get treatment, I don't know what would have happened. We might have just grown apart."

Some families do. John Willard, sixty-five, became depressed after his wife died. "I withdrew from everyone and just wanted to die. I was like that for two years, until one day I woke up and felt better. But by that time I had no friends left, and I hadn't seen my family very often. They were worried, but I told them to leave me alone. I hurt my daughter's feelings because I wouldn't let her help me. I said some awful things to her when I was at my lowest point. Things have never been the same since." His daughter concurred: "We were a lot closer before he became ill. He was so mean and angry during that time. He did and said things that hurt me so much I can't find forgiveness in my heart for him."

Often an emotionally disturbed individual affects other family members. Anxiety and depression are sometimes contagious diseases. Myra, thirty-two, is very concerned about her "nervous-wreck mother-in-law. She calls me three times a day from work to see how the baby is doing and has to be there at least once a day to see me nurse the baby. When I do things with the baby, she makes all kinds of faces and frightens me. I think that I am doing something wrong. When I know she is coming over, I get a pain in my chest and get stomach cramps. . . . She's making me like her!" A grandmother is concerned about her daughter's mental health. "How trustworthy is she with the baby? She tried to commit suicide when she was a teenager." Another grandmother worries that her ex-son-in-law, soon to be released from prison, will want to have custody of his two children, who live with her. "I took the kids after my daughter O.D.'d on heroin. Her husband is a dope addict and a thief. The kids lived like sewer rats with him. Now he is going to want them back." A mother complained that she is "worried sick" every time she visits her own mother because she doesn't know if she will find her drunk or sober. A grandparent has similar concerns; she is "worried sick because my daughter drinks during the time that she is at home with the kids. I have found her dead drunk several times with the baby crying in his crib."

Obviously, dealing with these problems requires a great deal of compassion and understanding. It is important, however, to remember that many of these problems are temporary and are amenable to treatment. People can change.

Two grandparents, the Powells, found this out. They learned this after experiencing a difficult period with their son-in-law, who, they complained, became "rude" and "short" to them the day after he started a new job. "I would come into the room to talk to him and he would go out another door," Mr. Powell said. "I really thought that he didn't like me. It hurt me, but I took it day by day." The fact was that his son-in-law, Matt, had become so preoccupied with his job that he was incapable of relaxing when he was away from work. He is a research engineer, an "egghead," as Mrs. Powell calls him, and was constantly ruminating about his research, oblivious at the time to how he was treating others. This went on for years until Matt left his research position for a different job. "The first day of his new job," Mr. Powell said, smiling, "he walked into my house, sat down at the kitchen table, and told me all about what he was doing. Ever since then, he is a totally different person and we get along famously. I never thought that it was his job that made him act like that. I thought that was the way he had become. I was ready to write him off."

Fortunately, Mr. Powell was flexible about the situation and didn't permanently write off his relationship with Matt during that difficult period. He was wise enough not to shun Matt. He persevered in the relationship and left the door open until Matt changed his behavior.

Mr. Powell's example teaches an important lesson: people shouldn't make permanent changes in their relationships because of problems that might be temporary. Anyone stressed by a difficult job situation, mental or physical illness, personal problems, or any number of difficulties can be difficult to deal with for a time, but can easily, like Matt, come to their senses when their circumstances improve. In relationships, it's important to be aware of what is happening on a day-by-day basis, to be flexible and patient, and to deal with difficulties in an open and forthright way.

Patience and flexibility isn't always the answer. Sexual abuse of children, according to some experts, is becoming more and more frequent. Certainly, people are increasingly more aware that it exists, especially its victims.

Nicole, thirty-two, is apprehensive about leaving her father alone with her little girl. "My sister and I were sexually abused by my father when we were youngsters. My father is wealthy and educated and travels around the world. How will my child understand when I won't let her go to the store with her grandfather alone, or allow him to take her to the zoo. I won't allow my daughter to go through what I did."

Whether she likes it or not, the best thing that Nicole can do is to talk to her father about it. If she is unable to talk to him alone, then she should discuss the situation with a close friend or seek professional help. In any case, she cannot ignore what's happening. If she does not confront her father, the situation will worsen until the tension thus created will either blow the lid off the situation or result in an unwilling grandchild-grandparent divorce. She would be doing her father a favor, too. Surely there is a part of him that regrets what he did. Bringing the issue out into the open is the first step in relieving the guilt and shame that he undoubtedly experiences. Most parents who have sexually molested their own children want to stop. When afforded an opportunity to unburden themselves of their own guilt and shame and confronted with their behavior, they are often relieved and eager to make amends. Bringing the problem out in the open and securing professional help quickly is the best way of bringing it to a halt. Keeping it under cover only leads to increasing emotional erosion, the infection of another generation, and the continuation of a painful past into a potentially happier present.

An increasing number of grandparents of children whose parents are divorced or cohabiting are concerned about sexual abuse of their grandchildren. When they suspect that their grandchildren are being abused or sexually molested by their new guardian or stepparent, some try to intervene, others try to gain custody of their abused grandchildren. But charges of abuse and sexual molestation are difficult to prove, and most grandparents are unsuccessful in their attempts to do anything about it short of removing their grandchild from the situation. When they do this, they not only flaunt the law but incur the wrath of the child's guardian and may be barred from further contact with their grandchildren.

Sandy Waltham, a sixty-five-year-old grandmother tried to obtain custody of her grandchildren from her ex-daughter-in-law, who "lives with a man who is a bum and molests the children. The children told me that he has them do 'sex' things to him. I noticed strange marks on their bottoms and bruises on their bodies. I told their pediatrician and called Welfare to investigate. Welfare said that everything was okay, but I know that it isn't. Now he won't let me near the kids. He hates me. What am I to do, just stand by and watch my little grandchildren be victimized?" Subsequently, she alerted her grandchildren's pediatrician and school principal, who have promised to keep a watchful eye over her grandchild and report any wrongdoing to the authorities.

WHEN MARRIAGES DISSOLVE

Two primary reasons for the end of a marriage are the death of a spouse, and divorce. After a divorce, a great deal of animosity often remains between former spouses, persisting even after the divorce is final. This pervasive anger easily infects all other family relationships, especially when family members have chosen sides in the divorce. Thus, ex-in-law relationships can be very precarious.

But when a spouse in a happy marriage dies, and the survivor remarries, there is no residual anger. Thus there is a good chance that the survivor will respect the children's relationship with their grandparents—if they also had a good relationship. That is the key.

When Cindy died of cancer at the age of thirty-four, her husband, Morris, became even closer to his in-laws. Cindy's parents were totally supportive of him and the children "in every way—financially, morally," he said. "They even let us live with them for a while. They understood my situation and encouraged me to marry again. I couldn't have asked for better friends and parents." When Morris remarried, he made it clear to his new wife that he would maintain his relationship with Cindy's parents, and his new wife readily acquiesed to his request. Cindy's father says, "I respect Morris. He knows that, through us, his children's mother is still alive. We lost Cindy, but not Morris. In fact, we like his new wife. She has become part of the family."

Most often, things don't go this smoothly. When a surviving spouse with a poor relationship to in-laws remarries, chances are that the in-laws will be eased out of their grandparenthood. This is a common fate of poor family relationships when marriages end, whatever the reason.

Many of today's grandparents can expect their children to divorce, and so they risk isolation from their grandchildren. No one knows how frequently this happens because people are reluctant to talk about it. Only recently has the extent of the issue become known, as thousands upon thousands of grandparents are flocking to the courts to gain access to their grandchildren. If their grandchild is legally adopted by a new stepparent, they find that their legal bond to the children is nonexistent.

Grandparents are deeply affected when their children divorce. Although most grandparents are not consulted when their child considers divorce, they are often recruited by their child to help after it occurs. Before the divorce, grandparents are stabilizing factors for children (and parents), and can offer them a sanctuary from the turmoil at home. After divorce grandparents of the child's custodian (custodial grandparents) are especially important. Studies show that there is a good chance that the available custodial grandparent, most often the maternal grandmother, will become closer to her grandchildren when divorce occurs. The noncustodial grandparents are in danger of being displaced. Other studies show that noncustodial grandparents can become more distant, but this is not an absolute rule.

When Lily, twenty-eight, divorced Sal, she and her children remained in her home, right next door to Sal's parents, the Garibaldis. "I love them and they are great. The kids love them. Why should I leave them because Sal's a creep? My parents live quite a distance away and they aren't half as interested in the kids as Sal's." Sal's mother feels that "Lily is like a daughter to me. Some people say that they lost a son or daughter through divorce. Not me. It's Sal's fault that they got divorced. I am ashamed of him. He couldn't stop carousing with his secretary and Lily couldn't take it anymore." Fortunately, the Garibaldis do not resent having to offer support to Lily as a single parent. Mrs. Garibaldi is generous. "I am home and I am available. I love the kids. Why not?" Mrs. Garibaldi is wise enough not to be blindly loyal to her son. To do otherwise would be to lose her beloved Lily. Her understanding and compassion has enabled her to maintain a loving relationship with them both.

Not everyone is as wise as Mrs. Garibaldi. Some grandparents can be short-sighted in recognizing the importance of a good relationship to their grandchildren's parents. Mr. and Mrs. Logan were unhappy because their ex-daughter-in-law was reticent about allowing visits with their grandchildren after she had divorced their son. "I love the kids and want to see them. My heart is broken," Mrs. Logan said. Linda, her daughter-in-law, complained that she didn't have time to worry about the Logans' problems. "I wouldn't care if the kids never saw them again. Anyway, it's not me they want or love. It's the kids. . . . I just come along with the kids." Linda has arrived at the crux of the issue: she comes along with the kids and "like it or not," as Mr. Logan said, "we are all stuck with one another and I am not in the driver's seat." If the Logans' don't work things out with Linda, they might lose frequent contact with their grandchildren, because the kids are aware of their attitude toward their mother.

It is important to emphasize the difficulty of these situations for the children. They are aware that if it were not for them, their elders would never have to see one another again. I have heard youngsters, over and over again, echo the words of Rachel, a twelve-year-old whose parents were involved in a bitter divorce: "If I were dead then my parents wouldn't have to talk to one another about me and my grandparents wouldn't have to talk to my mother to arrange to come over and see me. It would all be peaceful."

When marriages end, attention must be paid to safeguarding the emotional attachments of people other than the divorcing couple.

REMARRIAGE AND STEPGRANDPARENTING

Grandparents get divorced, too. For most parents and grandchildren it is a shattering experience when elders divorce after a long marriage. Everyone is adversely affected. Oftentimes the family is split in two as children and even older grandchildren take sides.

Lou, fifty-nine, and Stella, fifty-eight, divorced after thirty-five years of marriage because Stella just "didn't want to be married anymore." She had outpaced her husband in her career and was enjoying a great deal of approbation from her colleagues. She had "grown out of love with Lou" and wanted to "try it alone." Lou was "shocked and humiliated" by Stella's decision to divorce. "Everyone thought that we were the perfect couple," he said sadly. All of the family, their three children and six grandchildren, were angry with Stella. "How can she do this to us," her oldest son said, "at her age?" "I thought that she would settle down soon and enjoy her old age," her daughter said angrily. "Dad has been good to her. I love her too, but I am so damned angry at her. She has thrown the family for a loop. She goes out on dates. What the heck are we supposed to do on holidays?" "Do I have to choose between Grandma and Grandpa?" muttered Joey, their twelve-year-old grandson. "I seem to have lost my grandmother."

When grandparents remarry, things can get very, very complicated. They have to deal with their children's reaction to a "replaced" parent, in the case of death, or a new stepparent, in the case of divorce. It is not a simple task for, let us say, a parent with two children whose parents have divorced and remarried to deal with their parents, two new stepparents for themselves, and two new stepgrandparents for their children. Conflicts can arise when a parent disagrees with his or her parent's choice of a new spouse. The new spouse may be envious of the time and energy spent with the children and grandchildren. If these complex transitions are made smoothly, the children benefit because they have added to their list of possible vital connections. Unfortunately, problems are more often the case.

Many acquired stepgrandparents never get an opportunity to act in that role. In fact, remarried grandparents are often, in the words of Angie, whose father recently remarried, "lured away from the family." Angie was angry because "after all these years I was finally getting a chance to know my father. He retired from work and had plenty of free time. Then he ups and divorces my mother and moves in with a woman that was a family friend all of their lives. I hate her and won't ever talk to her. I don't want her near me or my kids. My father doesn't come around much anymore. She won't let him. She's got him by the nose. He's spending all his savings on her; that's money that he should be spending on his family. He's not very popular around here, to say the least. The kids used to adore him, now they make fun of him. They call him 'stud.'" Angie's father told me that he doesn't have time to spend with his "old family" because he needs time to "be with and get to know my new bride."

No one ever said it would be easy.

Competition arising between "real" grandchildren and stepgrandchildren in a reconstituted family for a grandparent's attention affects parents as well. Mrs. Roberts, seventy-two, has four "real" grandchildren and four stepgrandchildren that she inherited when her son married a widow who also had four children. Her daughter-in-law is angry with her because she favors her four grandchildren "publicly. I understand that she loves her own more, but it's the way that she does it. Christmas, for instance, she brings these lavish gifts for her own and some puny presents for mine. My kids just sit there and watch her grandchildren open her expensive gifts. It's terrible for them. They try to be nice to her, but that doesn't work. They resent the other kids because she likes them better." Mrs. Roberts is also perturbed. "What can I do? Why should I spend money on her kids? I didn't ask to be their grandmother. I've got enough of my own."

Mrs. Roberts would do well to remember that her stepgrandchildren aren't the enemy. They are only kids. Her favoritism is hurtful. She would do better by explaining to her own grandchildren that she will spend equally on all of the children. And they will love and respect her all the more for it—even though they may not exactly enjoy the loss of their favored treatment. Most kids are quite intuitive and understanding about things like this.

Steparents often complain that the demands of their stepchildren's grandparents are "too much." Willa, thirty-two, is exasperated. She "doesn't need the headaches with them" (her stepchildren's grandparents). "They call to see the kids. Who's got time for all this? I don't know if I did the right thing marrying a man with three kids. It isn't even the kids so much, it's the kids and those grandparents. It's too complicated." Her husband's ex-mother-in-law, Abbie Collins, is "desperate" about the situation. "Look here. Do you know what it is like to have your grandchildren in the keeping of a complete stranger! I am intimidated when I call. I feel like I'm bothering her. I don't blame her. It's no one's fault, it's the situation. I just don't know what to do. I feel extinct . . . disposed of. I know that I am losing the children, fading out of their lives. We don't share the same worlds anymore. I cry every night, and there is not a damn thing that I can do about it. Those kids are my life."

Mrs. Collins is right when she says that the situation is to blame, not the people. It should be regarded as the cost of doing business in divorce. An inordinately high degree of cooperation among family members is required for things to function even relatively smoothly. Respecting the diverse relationships among family members is in itself a challenge. Most of the responsibility for a happy outcome lies in the sometimes understandably reluctant hands of the remarried parents. Children and grandparents don't have much to say about the way things go, but grandparents certainly can help.

Mrs. Askin, fifty-six, decided on a strategy when her daughter died and her son-in-law remarried. "Rather than be a pain in the neck, I told myself to be a friend to my son-in-law's wife, Gina, and I did it. I see them often, and I go over every Saturday morning, like clockwork, with breakfast, and I help her any way I can with the kids." "She's great," Gina said, smiling. "She's a new friend, but she's better. She's also like a mother. My own kids are crazy about her. They really look forward to Saturday morning when she comes with bagels and lox and whitefish and cream cheese. She devotes her life to us. She is more involved with us than my parents or my husband's parents. But things don't always go smoothly. We have had a couple of disagreements, of course. Everyone does. But when something is bothering us, we talk about it. I said that from the very beginning, not to let things fester. If someone's got something on their mind, they should open their mouth about it. When anything's bugging me I sit down and talk it over with her. I can't even do that with my own mother. I lucked out when she came into my life."

How did Mrs. Askin come out on top in a potentially difficult situation?

She was faced with a choice when her son-in-law remarried: to fade away (like Mrs. Collins) or to decide what it was that she wanted to do and *do it!* Fortunately for her and her loved ones, she chose the latter alternative.

She was clear about what she did.

She assessed the situation: What was happening?

She pondered her options: What can I do about the situation?

She reflected upon the outcome of each option: What would

happen if I passively withdrew from my grandchildren? What would happen if I joined their new family?

She formulated a plan of action: "I will join the family and help as much as possible on a regular, respectful, and mutually convenient basis."

She established a support system, a policy of open communication that would ensure a healthy relationship. "When something's wrong, we talk it over." She taught other family members to communicate openly also. Gina talks to her more openly than she talks with her own mother. Members of the new generations can apply her method to their own family situations.

Broken families are vulnerable to conflicts, problems, and the estrangement of family members. Today, more and more family relationships are in jeopardy as broken families are becoming more numerous. According to the 1982 U.S. Census, the divorce rate hovers around fifty percent. Today more than one-quarter of all the families with children in the United States have only one parent present (this represents 25.7 percent of all family groups in 1985 as opposed to 12.9 percent in 1970). Grandparents are often the only stable unit within the broken family. Since there are some 12 million children not living with both parents, this means that approximately 24 million grandparents (assuming all are living) of children not living with their own parents have only a tenuous "vital connection" to their grandchildren. If we add to this the unknown number of parents who are feuding with their own parents, of children legally adopted away from grandparents, and of remarriages, etc., we arrive at the staggering figure that represents the number of children and grandparents whose "vital connection" is in danger of being totally lost—conservatively *over thirty million.*

The only way to prevent this from happening is to assure that family members openly and honestly communicate with one another from the time that the family is formed. If all family members have a direct relationship and are understanding of one another, they will ensure that the emotional attachment between grandparents and grandchildren will survive family feuds and even broken marriages. I cannot emphasize too strongly that it is incumbent upon grandparents to understand that their access to their own grandchildren depends greatly on the quality of their relationship to the child's parents, and in a broken marriage, to the child's custodial parent.

Grandparents should handle broken marriages with care. If they alienate the child's custodian, they are in danger of losing the grandchildren. A supportive, caring, and involved attitude, with open communication, is necessary. When Cindy died, her parents were wise enough to help Morris through his mourning, his acceptance of her death, and his eventual remarriage. They kept their grandchildren close by accepting their new stepmother and reconstituting their family. When Lily and Sal divorced, the Garibaldis kept their grandchildren close by loving and supporting their mother. It is incumbent upon parents and grandparents in broken families to work together.

For kids, stepparents and stepgrandparents start out as strangers. Children and grandparents, with no say in the matter, inherit one another. In the best of circumstances, all involved can gain a loving person. In the worst of circumstances, they are trapped with someone they learn to ignore or hate and who feels the same way about them.

Remarriage multiplies family obligations, and sometimes there is not enough time and attention to go around. Questions of priority arise. "Who comes first," a newly remarried father asked, "mine or hers or us or our parents?"

Most of the problems are not insurmountable. Something can be done about them if people are willing to work hard at doing it and to persevere in the face of initial frustration and discouragement. Although there are no quick remedies for soothing ailing families, plenty of help is available. With patience, things can be worked out. Mrs. Askin taught us that.

In the next chapter I will discuss a useful method for resolving troubles within the family. The method that I will describe can be adapted, in whole or in part, to most of the difficult situations that you might encounter.

FOURTEEN

Resolving Conflicts, Solving Problems

SOLVING FAMILY PROBLEMS

When a disagreement occurs, it is usual for the parties in contention to be defensive and each blame the other for the problem. It's a natural human reflex. Unfortunately, if both feuding parties are not mature enough to get past this stage of the conflict, nothing more happens and things inexorably get worse. Remember, there are no standoffs in family matters. If things don't get better, they get worse. Trained mediators and family therapists know that the secret of resolving conflicts is finding common interests among the quarreling parties, establishing a dialogue between them, and achieving a compromise concerning these interests. There is a tried and true method that people can use to work out their family problems. The new generation must learn this technique and use it. This method may be used individually, by a person desiring to resolve a conflict with another, or by a third party—a mediator or catayst—desiring to help reconcile conflicts between family members.

When a problem arises, the first thing to do is to ask the following questions:

1. What is happening? Assess the situation.
2. What options do I have to improve things?

3. What would result from acting on each option?
4. What is the best option?
5. How can I apply this option in the most effective manner?
6. What is the best way to discuss my plan with other family members?
7. What is the best way to monitor our progress?

When suffering a personal problem, the first thing to do is to examine your own attitudes and behavior to ascertain if they are helping or aggravating the situation. The next step is to put yourself in the other's place and "try on" the other's point of view. When you are unable to do this alone or don't want to but are distressing other family members, another person—a catalyst—must be recruited to help. The catalyst may be a family member, a friend, a clergyman, or a mental health professional. With a catalyst the situation can be resolved either alone—the third person talking to one of the parties—or in the context of a family conference where feelings are vented, each person's views are discussed, and a plan for reconciliation is agreed upon. Follow-up get-togethers are planned to keep things running smoothly.

Obviously, this isn't easy, especially considering the depth of emotions involved, the differences in personalities, and the diverse nature of the situations that can arise. But it can be done. The same method can solve family problems.

Here is a typical case of family conflict and its successful resolution, showing how one family worked out their differences.

A Family Problem

Marilyn Miller and her mother—we'll call her "Grandma"—were upset because Grandpa and Jon Miller, Marilyn's husband, had been ignoring one another ever since they "fell out" after the failure of a joint business venture. They almost came to blows over the matter, they blamed one another, and they did not take the time to attempt to understand the other's point of view. It concerned a sheep-raising and transporting business. Grandpa raised sheep and Jon sold them, transporting them to marketplaces around the country in a truck they jointly owned. Jon had accumulated a considerable amount of debt because of extensive repair bills on the truck. Unfortunately, he never told his father-in-law about the bills, until one day the truck was repossessed. Grandpa was thunderstruck and became very angry at Jon, accusing him of losing money on gambling and "blowing the whole business." Jon claimed that he "was sparing the old man all of the tension that I was going through. I didn't want to tell him how bad things were. I wanted to impress him and not disappoint him" and that "he is a terrible business man, unrealistic . . . pie in the sky." They lost their business as a result of the misfortune, and although each subsequently earned a good living, Grandpa as a ranch foreman and Jon as a building contractor, they continued their feud and shunned each other whenever they met. When open warfare ended, their communication broke down. They shunned one another and cemented themselves into a no-win stalemate.

Their conflict affected other family members. Marilyn was caught between her husband and her father. "Jon gets mad at me if I ever talk about Dad, even to the kids. He doesn't want his name mentioned here. He cared very much for my father and feels that Dad turned on him." Marilyn expressed a common theme that leads to a great deal of emotional turmoil in family feuds. When parents feel rejected by grandparents they once admired and respected, their sadness turns to vehement anger that severely impairs reconciliation. She continued, "Jon and I fight all of the time about this. It's affected our relationship. I am also angry at my father. You would think that both of them would have enough consideration for all of us to stop being so damned selfish and make up."

Marilyn's children, Jodie and Al, aged ten and eight, miss their grandfather. Jodie was sad. "Grandpa was always at the house. Now if we want to see him we have to go to their place, and it's far. Dad and Grandpa are making everyone unhappy because they are mad at each other. I can't say anything to Dad about Grandpa because he gets really mad. We used to all be happy and now everyone is uptight and it's no fun. My family is no fun anymore."

Marilyn's two brothers and sister and their children were also part of the conflict. Meg, Marilyn's sister-in-law, was angry at the "two muleheaded jerks, excuse the disrespect." Meg said that friends, neighbors, and merchants in their town knew what was going on. "It's an embarrassment to all of us."

Grandma was "put out, to say the least. I think that my husband would know better, that Jon wouldn't do him dirty on purpose. But he won't believe that. He really thinks that Jon didn't care about him and that Jon was dishonest. He is very hurt."

Grandpa agreed. "Damn right I am hurt. I couldn't believe that Jon would do that. All those bills. All of a sudden the business goes down the drain—with no warning. He was like a son to me."

Jon felt the same way. "Grandpa was more than a father to me. How could he think that I would do anything to hurt him. I just didn't want to tell him that the business wasn't working . . . I thought that I could pull it out of the fire for him, but it didn't work."

The problem at this point is that they couldn't tell each other what they were feeling. They were talking to intermediaries and shunning each other.

Grandma and Marilyn had "had it." They felt that the family had suffered enough because of Jon and Grandpa's feud. They, along with Meg, who is an involved family member, decided to "sit them down and talk it over." They decided to confront the situation, bring the parties together, and hold a family meeting.

Grandma confronted them both. She told them that not only were they suffering but that they were causing "everyone else to be miserable and that this "was enough." "You have something in common," she said, "*us.* So you have to work this out." Grandma served as the catalyst, the person who initiated the reconciliation procedure.

At the meeting, Marilyn pointed out how their behavior was affecting the family. "There were lots of tears. I told them how bad I felt and how the children were upset. Grandma told them that she was losing respect for them because they were selfish." Jodie was at the meeting, too, and told her father and grandfather how unhappy their conflict was making her.

Grandpa told me that Jodie convinced him that he had to do something about the feud. "She brought me up short. I never realized that she was so hurt by all this. I didn't really pay too much attention to my wife and Marilyn—well, except when they would cry."

Meg discussed their behavior. "Every time we have a get-together we are all tense. Everyone is looking at you both to see how you're getting along . . . if you're being nice to one another. Everyone is tense. After the get-together you both are the main topic of conversation: Did they talk to one another? Did they say hello or good-bye? These are questions that my own kids ask me."

The family made Jon and Grandpa confront each other with their own feelings and point of view. The shunning was ended.

Jon expressed his disappointment over Grandpa's reaction to his well-intentioned silence about the precarious state of their business. Grandpa expressed his anger and hurt about Jon's action and the loss of his relationship with Jon. With the family's prodding, they tried to see each other's point of view and understand why each had acted in the way that they did.

It worked. Jon and Grandpa, after hearing each other's points of view and arriving at the understanding that no malice was intended in either of their behaviors, decided to try to start over again. They agreed to let bygones be bygones, and shook hands. "Let's keep this out front so it doesn't happen again," Jon said. "If I've got something on my mind, you'll be the first to know about it, Grandpa." Jon had decided to nurture the relationship—to think about how it was going and to take action if a problem arose. "I know it'll never be like it was when we were close," Jon said sadly, "but it won't be as bad as when we were enemies, either."

A Useful Plan of Action to Settle Family Feuds

The Millers used a method to approach and solve the feud between Jon and Grandpa. Keep in mind, however, that this plan of action worked because of their "natural family arrangement"—their family contained members who wanted to be close to one another and were committed to family unity. Let's analyze what they did. Remembering these terms will help you to apply the method more easily to any family situation.

After the precipitating event that launched the feud, the failure of their business, Jon and Grandpa became involved in open warfare. They became angry at each other. The family became involved. Both Jon and Grandpa felt self-righteous about their positions and refused to consider the other's point of view. They became cemented in their own position. Their communication broke down. They stopped talking and began to ignore and shun each other. Their own discomfort decreased, but the discomfort of family members increased as their conflict contaminated the family. Their family became affected. Family members often take sides in feuds. At this point, the family established a secondary form of communication through intermediaries. When this was no longer tolerable someone—Grandma—decided to take matters into her own hands and settle the problem. A catalyst came forth, a strong family member who confronted the feuding parties, with or without the cooperation of other family members, concerning the effects of their behavior on the family. The catalyst or mediator explained the combatants' mutual interest—the family's well-being—and coerced the parties in the most creative way possible to re-establish communication and understanding by confronting each other in an attempt to iron out their problems. A reconciliation, in one form or another, was engineered and carefully monitored by the catalyst, who had become, for a time anyway, the family-appointed guardian of the relationship.

Grandma Miller and Marilyn did this for their family. To this date, Jon and Grandpa are, in Jodie's words, "a lot better."

Members of the new generation embroiled in family problems can serve as catalysts and apply this method to work things out among family members. Don't be shy about intervening. When family members feud, sit them down and talk out the problems. Don't give up until a reconciliation is achieved.

SOLVING PERSONAL CONFLICTS

Some people's first instinct is to try to ignore problems and use avoidance, a mild form of shunning, as a way to deal with their feelings. This doesn't work because of the intertwined nature of the family: no one acts alone. Family members naturally affect one another. When a conflict arises, it should be dealt with quickly.

The ability of an individual to deal with an emerging problem depends primarily on his or her personality and personal style. People who are in touch with their feelings and open and relaxed about communicating their feelings to others are able to nip family problems in the bud. Others who are reserved and reticent about communicating with others find it difficult to identify, confront, and work out problems.

The following scenario illustrates this.

Mary is a shy and formal thirty-one-year-old mother of four who finds that she is beginning to dread her in-laws' visits. They come twice a year, for one week at a time. When they arrive, her husband and her children are happy to see them, but she isn't. Mary doesn't know why she feels this way, and feels guilty about it because everyone around her seems happy. In reality, her feelings are a signal that something is wrong. By judging her feelings and blaming herself, she is ignoring this important warning. Something really is wrong with the situation.

Mary notices that she is isolating herself from family activities, either by drifting away from the center of family activity or by "not feeling well." Because Mary doesn't "look well," and acts withdrawn, her husband wonders what is wrong and the children, sensing their mother's discomfort, begin to get unruly. Her in-laws begin to think that Mary doesn't want them around. Because nothing is said, everyone's imagination takes over and, naturally, imagines the worst. Mary's in-laws, the Lantons, begin to feel tense and self-conscious. Her husband, Rick, begins to get irritable, caught between his wife's increasing aloofness and his parents' unexpressed concern. The atmosphere in the house gets increasingly tense, until the Lantons find an excuse to leave early.

If Mary were able to use her thoughts as a signal and say to herself, "Let me find out what's wrong," she would find that she resents the topsy-turvy state her home gets in after the Lantons arrive. Not only does she have to remove one of the children from his room to make a place for her in-laws, but her normal—and very busy—routine is disrupted by having to cater to her in-laws' needs in her formal and dutiful style, a rigidity that is unnecessary under the circumstances. Her husband does not help her because he is working. He gets a great deal of pleasure spending time with his parents when he returns home . . . while Mary cooks. Mary's difficulty arises because she is a dutiful and respectful person who finds it hard to delegate authority, feels that she has to do it all herself—perfectly—and resents it. Thus she declines her in-laws sincere offers to help her with the work and her husband's offer to take them out to restaurants more often. He silently thinks that she is a "martyr." She grudgingly refuses to share the burden but isn't aware of it. If Mary wanted to help herself, she could do the following:

1. Examine her behavior.
2. Find the reasons for her behavior. Why am I behaving like this? This done, Mary must ask herself:
3. What am I doing to contribute to the situation? When she has satisfied herself as to the nature of the problem and the part she plays in the situation, it is time to sit down and talk things over with her family and:
4. Communicate. If Mary is able to do this things will work out. She can:
5. Make a plan.

Mary would find that her in-laws would be happy to visit for a shorter period of time, or to spend some of the visit in an inexpensive motel so Mary's home life would not be disrupted. If Mary were a bit more flexible, she would allow the family to eat out more often and not feel obliged to cook elaborate meals. She would take her husband up on his offer to take his parents and the children away for the day, to give her a rest. If Mary was unable to identify and confront the situation, she would have no alternative but to become increasingly upset and to eventually discourage her in-laws' visits without them ever knowing why, or being given an opportunity to help. This is the fate of many parent-grandparent conflicts.

Using this method as a guide, I have devised a simple checklist that any parent or grandparent can use to help them address their own family problems or those of other family members. I will use Mary's situation to illustrate how the checklist can be used.

Ten Steps to Take in Family Problems

1. Assess the situation. What's happening? Who is involved? (Mary was unhappy about her in-laws' visit.)
2. What is the status of the problem—Open warfare, shunning, or estrangement? (Mary was shunning her company, isolating herself.)
3. What are the stories and attitudes of people involved in the problem? (Mary felt tired, angry, overburdened, and misunderstood.) If you are directly involved, assess your own feelings, thoughts, and behavior. Are you helping or hurting the situation? (Mary was hurting the situation because she was not open with her feelings or direct in her communications.) Could you do better? If you can, what's stopping you? (Mary's personal style and personality impaired her from expressing her feelings.)
4. Talk to other family members and get their opinions. Try to understand everyone's point of view by pretending that you are an attorney defending their case. (Mary couldn't do this because she was guilty about her feelings and unable to be objective about them, to use her feelings as information. She chose to "judge" them instead.)
5. Analyze the components of the problem according to the categories in this book. Are the problems caused by different lifestyles, personalities, or attitudes? Are there role reversals, insensitivity, abandonment? (In Mary's case, people were insensitive to the work that their visit required of her. On the other hand, she never asked them to cooperate.)
6. Define the common interests of the parties involved. (Mary wanted a happy family.)
7. Using common interests, think about helpful options for work-

ing out the existing problems. (Mary had many options available once she was able to discuss the problem openly.)

8. Formulate a plan using common interests and the best options available. (Mary and her family got together to discuss what could be done.)
9. Communicate your plan directly to the party or parties involved. Discuss the plan, and use your plan as a start to develop a working plan that all parties will agree to honor.
10. Carry out the plan. (The Lantons moved to a nearby hotel, the family ate out more often, and Rick spent time alone with his parents so Mary could have time for herself.) Have frequent meetings with all of the involved parties to monitor, discuss, and improve the plan when necessary.

These ten steps make for a convenient personal checklist with which to plan and implement an approach to solving most of the feuds and personal vendettas that can arise within families. Working out conflicts before they become major problems is especially helpful in analyzing the difficulties family members have relating to one another in terms of roles, authority, burden, responsibility, obligations, etc. The common difficulties that I have enumerated—in-law troubles, too much or too little grandparenting, insensitivity, spoiling, etc.—can be helped quickly by early identification, confrontation, communication, discussion, resolution, and monitoring. To do this, family members must be open with their feelings and communicate freely with one another directly, without intermediaries. They, and especially the elders, must put themselves in the other person's shoes and attempt to look at the situation through the other's eyes. Avoid defensive positions. Ignore who is right or wrong, and define your common interests.

These are the emotional tools that the new generation must learn how to use, and use well, so they can keep their families happy and healthy.

FIFTEEN

Agenda for the New Generations: Let Your Family Begin Again

To let the family begin, parents and grandparents need one another. Exactly what do they need?

Parents need grandparents to guide their family, to teach and to nurture them. They need elders to stand aside and allow them to exercise authority in their own domain, using their own parents as gentle and noncritical advisors. Parents need love, praise, and respect from their elders for all they are doing. They need support, consideration, and admiration for persevering under the enormous burdens placed upon them by the way life is lived today. They need grandparents to be available to them and their children in just the right way —"on call" not too much, not too little. They need grandparents to be flexible, to stand in for them when necessary, and to step back when requested. Most of all, they need the grandparents' good example. I hope that some of the people in this book have provided that.

Grandparents need love and respect from their children also. They want their children to understand their need for some degree of "apartness," a time to rest, and a time to be involved in other things. They need the parents to understand that they need their grandchildren as a source of joy and emotional sustenance. They want parents to know that sometimes it's hard to relinquish authority and to change roles, to be a parent one moment and a grandparent the next. They want respect for their own history, their own ways, and the past in which they lived. They need support from their children, and to know that their children are there when they need them. They want to be a part of their lives. They need their children to be close when they get older and prepare to die.

Grandchildren need it all.

The mandate for the new generation of parents and grandparents entering the scene is to create a life view and a world in which they can fulfill one another's needs and pass on the emotional bounty that each generation accrues. The new generations will have to relinquish selfish attitudes—the "me" and the ethic of "doing my own thing" that predominates today. New parents and new grandparents will have to, as one child said, "be grown-ups," to think of others first and sacrifice personal comfort, finances, and time for the good of their families. They need to dedicate themselves to sticking together and working out their problems. Altruistic people will find this easy, but others not so naturally inclined will have to fight hard to protect their families against a society that advocates individualism, narcissism, and separation. In today's world, emotional bonds, for many, are equated with emotional bondage. The new generation will have to be creative and throw away the social script they have inherited. They must recognize their past familial experience—whether it was average, wonderful, or terrible—as information and emotional learning that can enhance their present and future. They must dedicate their resources to making their present family arrangement as close to the ideal as possible. Their purpose must be to forge a family arrangement that works now and that will be a source of strength and comfort for the generations to follow.

One of the most challenging obstacles is physical distance: we are a mobile people. Family members are constantly on the move, searching for something better, and ending up settling great distances from one another. This can be devastating. New parents and grandparents will have to do the best they can to find creative and innovative ways of solving the problems of distance. It's important for grandparents to be present when new grandchildren come along, supporting the parents as well as enjoying the new baby. To counter the harmful effects of distance on their relationship, some call their grandchildren frequently, send notes, family newsletters (one headline read "Matthew gets good grades on report card"), pictures, videotapes, and homemade gifts. Others record their family history, have frequent family get-togethers, invite children along on vacations, and even take vacations with their grandchildren. Many are ingenious. One grandparent I know reads stories into a tape recorder and sends them to her distant grandchildren to listen to at bedtime or on long car trips. Another runs a summer camp for her grandchildren at her own home. Where there is a will, there is a way.

Another challenge facing the new generations is balancing work time and family time. This is especially important for today's women, especially homemakers who have raised their children and are now—many for the first time—entering the work force. The time and commitment involved in work often leaves little energy for the families. The emotional cost to children has yet to be assessed. The new generation of older women workers, recently emancipated from the limited options that their society offered them, may be in danger of spending too much of their energies in their newfound work environment and effectively ignoring their grandmotherhood. The same holds for men, who, as I have emphasized, have a golden opportunity to be with children, perhaps for the first time in their lives, as they near retirement age. Will the members of the new generations be wise enough to take advantage of this opportunity, or will they stay in the same limited rut of the work world. Or will they just take off to retire?

More of the same isn't the answer for the new generations. It behooves newly liberated elders to stay put, instead of retiring to a far-off place. They should apportion their family, work, education, rest, solitude, and recreation time in a flexible and balanced fashion. Part-time retirement is okay, and part-time work is okay, because it affords elders the flexibility to be available regularly and in emergencies for their families. How can grandparents who work full-time attend school plays, athletic events, or even birthday celebrations in which their grandchildren star? How can they play in the snow with their grandchildren or help with a new arrival if they never leave the confines of the "sun belt"? Full-time anything is a trap that elders must avoid. It isolates them from their families and from the process of life itself. Remember, time together is the basic ingredient of the vital connection, as well as of all emotional attachments.

Another issue is the dark side of the gift of longevity. More and more, grandparents and great-grandparents will be increasingly dependent on their families for life support—and for a long time. The unavoidable obligation to care for their parents places the middle generation in the difficult position of supporting their parents and children at the same time. Even if parents delegate the day-to-day operation of this responsibility to paid strangers or social institutions, they are ultimately responsible for supervising, administrating, and paying or arranging payment for the care of their aging parents. Parents have little choice in the matter; the question is not if they want to do it but rather how to do it the best way possible. The willingness of the middle generations to suffer this burden and their attitude in carrying it out is directly related to how much they love and value their elders.

Does this tell us something concerning how the new generations should prioritize their lives? Hopefully, members of the new generations will be alert to the fact that a long and possibly lonely future awaits them in their later years after their friends die, and will look for satisfactions within their families. Healthy elders have got to become involved. Now is the time when young parents and children need their dedication and support. Of what use to society are elders who have retired full-time away from the mainstream? What can they expect from the people they have abandoned but to be abandoned themselves? Why should financially struggling parents support their elders if their elders failed to support them when they were able?

Fortunately, there is a good answer to these questions: the new generations should make their children and grandchildren the highest priority in their lives. Only in this way will they become truly beloved and useful and vital while still having plenty of time to do whatever else pleases them. They won't die alone and lonely, like so many people who have spent their lives within a similar age group. By doing this, they will have put down roots into other generations. I have witnessed many instances where elders who have loved and nurtured their young were loved and cared for by them personally in their old age. They died, as one young farmer's wife described her grandmother's death, in the "back bedroom of my house." Where do the new generations want to die? With whom, family members or paid strangers? How much will they be willing to devote their lives to their families now in order to die among them later?

The seeds of a good family life are planted in the emotional soil of the parent-child relationship and are tended by devoted grandparents. Indeed, I can conclusively say that grandparents—first as parents but most importantly as grandparents—are responsible for the way a family is. As grandparents go, so goes the family. Grandparents set the example and show the way for their children and their grandchildren. Good grandparents beget good parents, who beget good children and grandchildren, and future parents and grandparents.

Whether it is perceived as a privilege or a burden, nature has bequeathed the awesome responsibility of showing the way to grandparents. Those entering their later years must heed this carefully. The quality of their future is rooted not in isolation or places, but in people: their family. Many elders prefer to live exclusively among their friends and age peers, but this is a mistake. This attachment can be limited by commitment and age. It's not a good idea to put all of one's emotional eggs in one old basket. They are better placed in many baskets, especially with family, as well as friends, where the attachment is deep and where people of all ages enhance and amuse one another. The new generation must search out the young people, not only in their family but in schools, communities, religious life, and so on. That's where the real action is. That's where life is. That's where the fun is.

Today's grandparents and grandparents-to-be have an important role in public life. Because of their age and position, they are currently running most of society's businesses and institutions. It is imperative that they, along with their younger colleagues, begin to adopt an intergenerational view in their daily lives, and to do something to mesh the generations in the world that they touch. The possibilities are infinite.

In education, elders should be an integral part of the daily school life of children. In the military, grandparents should be afforded the opportunity to visit their grandchildren at least once while they are doing an overseas tour of duty. Helping professions should include children in nursing homes and senior programs, as well as promoting elders' involvement with children in hospitals, residential centers, and outpatient clinics. Religious institutions should be acutely aware of the power of elders in transmitting religious values and ways, and aggressively and creatively foster the vital connection between members of their religious communities. Businesses should respect the grandparent-grandchild bond as it does the parent-child bond. Allow grandparents a generous leave of absence when a new grandchild comes along. Government must pay attention to the myriad possibilities of spicing up various programs by peppering them with people of all ages.

Start now to think about and begin to involve people of all ages with one another. It won't be easy; institutions easily become set in their ways and resistant to change. Fortunately, people control institutions, and many of these people are grandparents. If you are a grandparent, start *now* to mesh the generations together. If you are a parent, urge the elder-in-charge, your occupational superior, to adopt the intergenerational viewpoint at the workplace. Make it happen!

I believe that the new generations of parents and grandparents, if they heed these suggestions, can make an emotional revolution happen and make life richer and more satisfying than ever before.

They have learned a great deal from the past decades of social and technological changes and its effect upon their emotional lives. Hopefully, they will not perpetuate the emotional carnage that attended this so-called progress. Hopefully, they will have learned from their personal mistakes and the folly of their culture. Hopefully, they will not have been so bruised by prior negative family experience that they have banished the idea of family from their lives. Hopefully, they will make this emotional revolution in their lives, reinstate the birthright of their grandchildren to a close relationship with them, and leave a legacy of a better world to their descendants.

Nature offers abundant opportunities to do so. With every child that is born, the new generations have another chance to fulfill their birthright and to prepare a legacy for their descendants. It's as simple as that.

Appendix

Grandparents' Rights

While we were doing our research, we came across a different category of grandparents. Unlike many others, they were angry and upset because they couldn't see their grandchildren often enough. Many of them were deprived because the child's custodian—sometimes their own children—wouldn't allow them to visit, especially in the event of a death, divorce, or separation.

In 1975, few grandparents had legal recourse, and some were being permanently legislated out of access to their grandchildren. Little consideration was ever given to the needs of the grandchildren. Since that time, we have met and corresponded with thousands of grandparents and many parents who have shared their sides of the controversy with us. The emotional carnage in these cases is horrendous. Recently, because of a concerted effort by grandparents all over the country (especially Lee and Lucille Sumpter of Haslett, Michigan) and the new knowledge about the critical importance of the grandparent-grandchild relationship, there are now laws in forty-nine states that give grandparents the right to petition the courts in order to see their grandchildren. More and more are winning visitation rights, and are even reconciling their families, since the judiciary has begun to recognize the indispensable nature of this attachment. But a day in court does not automatically win the case. When a child is adopted by strangers or a child's custodian remarries, natural grandparents are routinely shunted aside and pushed out of the family portrait. With a highly mobile population and an astronomical divorce rate, this disastrous occurence is not unusual. Courts are not the answer. Prevention and mediation are the best options in these situations.

THE FOUNDATION FOR GRANDPARENTING

What did our study show that could help us to formulate the purpose and goals of the Foundation?

The good news from our study was that, indeed, a "vital connection," a unique and complex emotional attachment, existed between grandparents and grandchildren. The sad news was that the majority of grandparents and grandchildren that we met did not have vital connections. What we found was a majority of people who were emotionally isolated from one another: hard-working parents, busy with keeping their lives intact; alienated elders, willing or—less often—unwilling, but having little to do with their grandchildren; and a legion of children being raised by "paid strangers" and social institutions.

This led us to the decision to develop an organization that would teach and demonstrate, through projects and programs, the importance of the vital connection and the value of an intergenerational society. Our goal would be to raise people's consciousness about the role of grandparenting as an important stage of life and to demonstrate that, as we learned from our study, the natural role of the elder is emotional work—the application within the family and community of the wisdom and experience the elder has accumulated over years. Our goal would be to disprove the current ageist attitudes that relegate elders to the limited options of joining the role of the nameless and alienated aged or continuing to stay in the work world.

We embarked on an educational campaign to alert people about the importance of these issues. We started a Grandparent Network and Grandparent Hotline, and published a newsletter entitled *Vital Connections* in order to coordinate and facilitate communication among individuals interested in making changes in their communities. We held workshops and meetings around the country in order to bring these issues before the public. The Grandparents' Rights issue attracted a great deal of public attention and stirred many people to assess the state of emotional health of their own families in order to prevent its dismemberment.

Today the fields of law, religion, education, and mental health are re-examining their perceptions and their attitudes toward intergenerational issues. Scholars, in ever increasing numbers, are becoming more interested in examining the grandparent-parent-grandchild relationship. A national Grandparent Day has been established, and grandparents are being invited to schools more frequently in the Grandparents Day In the Schools Program. Some children are routinely spending time in nursing homes as a part of their school day, and clever people are thinking up innovative intergenerational programs at an increasing rate.

The Foundation is developing an educational Expectant Grandparent Program, to be included in currently existing childbirth education programs. In this program, grandparents would be included in the prepartum, delivery, and postpartum periods of the birth of their new grandchild. We feel that this time, when the new baby comes on the scene, is the time for people to start thinking about establishing the three-generational family. The program is designed not only to teach people about how grandparents, parents, and children might operate, but to deal with personal issues in order to prevent family disruption. This book will be an integral part of this program, helping people to do things right at the start rather than to spend boundless time and energy having to undo years of hurt and resentment.

The growing interest in grandparenting is evidenced by the great deal of mail that the Foundation receives just from grandparents. An increasing number of letters from parents and even grandchildren are received daily. The contents of these letters not only deal with the problems and pain in the relationship but also include joyful proclamations of happy times and portraits of fine people, as well as creative suggestions for enriching family life and bridging the gaps caused by distance and other factors.

Because the bond between the young and the old is such an important part of one's life experience, there is no reason that people without biological relatives two generations away should be deprived of this experience. Thus, the Foundation is examining ways to extend the grandparenting role beyond that of biological grandparents to include individuals who, for one reason or another, do not have biological grandchildren or grandparents. We believe that all elders should have at least one youngster to be "crazy about," and vice versa. Grandparenting supplies the role model for a healthy and fulfilling old age. And grandchildren want grandparents.

For information write:

Foundation for Grandparenting
Box A
Jay, New York 12941

Bibliography

Concha, Joseph. "Grandfather and I." *The Way: An Anthology of American Indian Literature,* edited by F.A. Witt. New York: Alfred A. Knopf, Inc., 1972.

Cronin, A.J. *The Green Years.* Boston: Little, Brown and Co., 1944.

de Beauvoir, Simone. *The Coming of Age.* Paris: Editions Gallimard, 1970.

Denise, Paulme, ed. *Women of Tropical Africa.* Berkeley: University of California Press, 1963.

Deutsch, Helene. "The Psychology of Women." *Motherhood,* vol. II. Orlando, Florida: Grune and Stratton, 1945.

Fairlie, Henry. "Too Rich for Heroes." *Harper's* (November 1978).

Fortes, Martin. "Ritual Festivals." *American Anthropologist* (1936).

Gutman, David L. "Deculturation and the American Grandparent." *Grandparenthood,* edited by Bengston & Robertson. Beverly Hills: Sage Press, 1985.

Hagestad, Grunehild O. "Continuity and Connectedness." *Grandparenthood,* edited by Bengston & Robertson. Beverly Hills: Sage Press, 1985.

Knopf, Olga. "The Facts and Fallacies of Growing Old." *Successful Aging.* New York: Viking Press, 1975.

Kornhaber, Arthur and Kenneth L. Woodward. *Grandparents/Grandchildren: The Vital Connection.* New York: Anchor Press/Doubleday, 1981.

Kornhaber, Arthur. "Grandparents: The Other Victims of Divorce." *Reader's Digest* (February 1983).

———. "Teenagers and Grandparents." *Seventeen* (August 1983).

Mead, Margaret. "Growing Old in America." *Psychology Today* (March 1980).

Minturn, L.A. and W.W. Lambert. *Mothers of Six Cultures: Antecedents of Child Rearing.* John Wiley and Sons, 1964.

Neisser, Edith. "How to Be a Good Mother and Grandmother." Public Affairs Pamphlet no. 174, 6th edition, 1956.

Parsons, Talcott and Robert F. Bales. *Family: Socialization and Interaction Process.* New York: Free Press, 1952.

Troll, Lillian E. "The Contingencies of Grandparenting." *Grandparenthood,* edited by Bengston & Robertson. Beverly Hills: Sage Press, 1985.

United States Department of Health, Education and Welfare. "The Older Person in the Home."

Wilson, Edward O. *On Human Nature.* Cambridge, Mass.: Harvard University Press, 1978.